THE TRAIL
TO
LEADERSHIP

SECURING AMERICA'S FUTURE ONE BOY AT A TIME

QUINT AVENETTI

The Trail to Leadership
Copyright © 2018 by Quint D. Avenetti

ISBN (Print Edition): 978-1-54392-331-5
ISBN (eBook Edition): 978-1-54392-332-2

Jacket design by Bookbaby

To my three sons: Quint, Gunner and Cannon

no father could be more proud of his sons who have proven

that application of sound moral principles and a firm value system

will produce the strong American men our country deserves.

I wish you a wife as wonderful as your mother,

children as wonderful as you are and a life as rich as I have enjoyed.

To my lovely wife who has endured countless deployments and wars

where she juggled the boys, the household and always held firm on

team parenting. Good men truly come from strong women.

CONTENTS

	Prologue	9
Chapter 1	Setting the Stage	11
Chapter 2	On Courage	21
Chapter 3	On Integrity	26
Chapter 4	On Humor	30
Chapter 5	On Situational Awareness	33
Chapter 6	On Respect	38
Chapter 7	On Perseverance	41
Chapter 8	On Selflessness	45
Chapter 9	On Fear	51
Chapter 10	On Initiative	56
Chapter 11	On Accountability	59
Chapter 12	On Failure	62
Chapter 13	On Patriotism	65
Chapter 14	On Citizenship	68
Chapter 15	On Honor	73
Chapter 16	On Mind, Body & Spirit	98
Chapter 17	On Humility	104
Chapter 18	On Forgiveness	107
Chapter 19	On Vision	109
Chapter 20	On Loyalty	113
Chapter 21	On Adversity	117
Chapter 22	On Choices	120
Chapter 23	On Energy	124
Chapter 24	On Empathy	130
Chapter 25	On Boldness	133
Chapter 26	On Optimism	136
Chapter 27	On Leadership	139
	Epilogue	144
	Bibliography	146

PROLOGUE

The fight had been on for weeks, chow consisted of Meals Ready to Eat (MREs) for days on end and for a brief period, one MRE per Marine daily would be our subsistence as logistics trains bringing resupplies would rightfully prioritize ammunition and fuel into the fight. Finally word spread that hot chow would be arriving in the position. The Marines were battle weary but the prospect of hot chow brought a smile to their faces. When the trucks finally arrived Marines automatically lined up without a word, the lowest ranking Leathernecks first in line followed by the non-commissioned officers and then the older grizzled staff non-commissioned officers and lastly the commissioned officers. There is no need to shout out orders as to sequencing, all Marines are taught this from day one of Marine Corps Boot Camp and Officer Candidate School; leaders eat last.

The grimy faced, tired warriors seem always to be starving and chow time is always greeted by field Marines with a hunger unequalled by a bear after hibernation. When all the Marines have made it through the line the Commander and Sergeant Major gaze around to ensure no stragglers have been missed and that meals have been prepared for those Marines attending to duty and unable to come to chow in person. Once convinced that all have eaten, the commander and Sergeant Major finally step up to the serving line to partake in what is now no longer hot chow and far from plentiful. Very often the chow runs out and the senior Marines are left to enjoy the delicacies of yet another MRE. This process plays out at every Marine command, in every unit and at every level, even when only two Marines are getting chow, the senior Marine will always place the junior Marine before him in line without a word being spoken; leaders eat last. This very simple gesture, while tribal in nature, lays out the moral true north for a culture of leaders, a culture of winners and the Father-Son, Teacher-Scholar approach to building our next generation of American leaders, leaders who will secure this great experiment in democracy we call the United States of America.

CHAPTER 1

SETTING THE STAGE

In my years as a Marine, raising my three sons and working as a Boy Scout Leader, I have seen the product of good mentoring and training as well as the disappointment of neglecting the character development of young boys and its impact on their growth into young men. Now more than ever, we see that society has encroached on the male identity and created a gap so to speak in how we mentor our young boys into young men. In effect, society is seeking to re-define what we have historically and culturally come to know as young American men. There has been an assault of late on the value system that created the Greatest Generation, the same system that led to victory in two World Wars, the development of such iconic leaders as George Washington, Patrick Henry, Abraham Lincoln, Teddy Roosevelt, Ronald Reagan, Generals Black Jack Pershing, George S. Patton, Douglas McArthur and James N Mattis to name a but a few. There has been an erosion of traditional values, American values and our children are being told that they can be whichever gender they identify with on that particular day. The lines between right and wrong are becoming increasingly blurred by societal pressures with integrity taking a back seat to convenience and personal gain.

Our country will only remain strong so long as men of character are willing to stand on principle and support the value system that made our nation so great. These men don't simply appear, they must be nurtured, mentored and preened to peak performance regardless of background, environment or personal situation. Our young boys deserve the opportunity to become the men that our country expects, the men that our communities expect, the men that our families expect and the men that place honor and character as anchors of behavior, ethical decision making, superior performance, and humility in success. We are led to believe by the cultural elite that heroes are those who excel on the field of athletics, the stage of pop art, music or the screens of Hollywood and if we don't correct this now, we will watch the very fabric of this great nation ripped to shreds.

We see grown men devoid of respect for their nation because they have no idea of the sacrifices made by those who came before them to guarantee them those freedoms of "misplaced behavior" they so ungraciously flaunt in the revered name of free speech. Young boys now emulate such behaviors as heroic because no one is there to teach them otherwise. We see the erosion of inner city youth where minorities often lack a male father figure or worse yet, a good male figure period, and a life of crime and violence as the path most often travelled. More often than ever, we see families split apart and the traditional family value system degraded where in most cases mothers now have to be both father and mother. We see the proliferation of terrorism and the disturbing notion that such behavior is an option our boys may contemplate much less actually choose. It used to be that athletics was a path towards disciplined action, team before self, and humility in victory and prayer in thanks. These values are under attack by those ultra-liberal few, those cultural elites, who cry the loudest to ban prayer and religion from the public regardless of the overwhelming majorities' strength. Political correctness has sewn the lips of all but the boldest for fear of reprisal. To be sure the speed of information flow in today's world bridges time and space like no time in history and this plays into the hands of those who would infer their misled passions on we silent but powerful majority.

It has been said that the ancient Spartan warriors were selected not by their physical prowess rather, by the strength of the women in their lives. They were selected based on the inner strength and resolve of their mothers and wives and I personally am an advocate for such thought as I was blessed to have both mother and wife of extraordinary strength. Most significantly, I have the utmost respect for mothers raising a young boy on their own, say nothing of raising multiple children on their own. Allow me to clarify, my regard is for those single mothers who actually actively partake in the development of their children, not those who abrogate their development to their social environment or cultural influences. Many single mothers will understandably opt for the easy way out and claim to be too busy and too tired to put the extra effort into building the foundational base we hope to see in our boys. In my experience as a Scoutmaster I have had the privilege of knowing many single moms who have not only made the extra effort in supporting their boys in scouting as well as other extra-curricular activities, but have also actively participated as adult volunteer leaders. My point; this is too important, and it can be done, and I take my hat off to those single moms who have invested in their son's futures, these ladies are the mettle from which greatness evolves.

The development of a young man should take into account the median as well as the extremes of the human spirit, not as binding limits rather as an analysis of motivations, human characteristics, psychological impacts and the nature of development. Very few events in life provide us with the opportunity to examine the human spirit on such a broad spectrum more than armed conflict. There are several occasions at the ends of the spectrum which also provide opportunity to delve into the extremes of the human psyche such as extreme sports which challenge the extent of the individual spirit or at the opposite end, those individuals faced with life struggles due to severe illness such as many cases of cancer. I have had opportunity to examine close hand; combat as a United States Marine for 28 years and the fight for life of many cancer patients most notably and recently my mother. Armed with these experiences, an amazingly wonderful ten years as an adult leader working with young boys in the Boy Scouts of America, and no small amount of research, I will attempt to convey an approach that you may be able to relate to and perhaps apply in your own journey with your sons.

There is not, nor is this intended as an authoritative book on raising children as every child is made up of different DNA and unique in the beauty of God's hand. Some have buttons that respond easily to positive stimulation while others require a much more involved and studied approach to elicit positive response. We grow up, marry, have children and then figure it out on the go, hoping we can succeed with the least amount of failure. We joke that the first child is the experiment, where we figure out how it's done. In today's society more than ever we find our children influenced by social media and the seemingly instantaneous access to information (good, bad or otherwise) and we struggle to stay ahead of these unsavory influences. The young, teenage American boy is challenged to grow up with the same or similar ideals we did in our pre-access generation yet every voice on social media is quick to pass judgment on every aspect of his life. This book will tell a tale, offer some anecdotes and attempt to present some food for thought in raising a young boy to be a young man of character, moral values and an ethical decision making process. These foundational attributes or building blocks will point your son to moral true north and put him on the trail to leadership and a life of success and joy.

I must admit that I am not a child psychologist or social worker with a resume' of saved lives or salvaged futures. I am also in no way an expert in raising young girls as I have three sons and no daughters. You will find this book focuses on boys however, you may also find that many of the lessons and advice in this book will work just as well for young ladies as young men and I encourage you to use these methods if you so choose, but I must place a disclaimer on my lack of experience with our young ladies. Accordingly, throughout this book I will use the masculine reference and ask your indulgence in exchange for what I believe to be some interesting anecdotes, very important lessons and humble advice. Before asking you to trust in my advice and believe in my methods I suppose I should give a short account of my history as a precursor to laying out my case for our next generation of leaders and men.

I am the product of small town immigrant America, the son of an Arizona Copper Miner by way of service in our nation's military during the Korean era (U.S. Marine Corps and U.S. Army). My father came out of the Marine Corps in 1956 and started work in the Copper Mines where he met my mother, the youngest daughter of Mexican immigrants whose father had passed when she was an infant and her two eldest brothers were away fighting the Germans in Europe. My father asked my mother's eldest brother, a veteran of World War II and now the patriarch of his 9 siblings for her hand in marriage. My mother's other brother would return from the war in Europe draped under the American flag. Once married my father decided to return to military service and joined the Army where he became a paratrooper in the 101st Airborne Division and a stint at Ft. Campbell Kentucky.

My early childhood home was in the Mexican American immigrant neighborhood of San Pedro, Arizona. The home I first remember was a wood and adobe house built into the side of a steep hill, a very small yard and a few dogs as pets. Much of San Pedro was either directly related on my mother's side or one or two places removed by marriage and considered as family. In this small community my peers almost exclusively spoke Spanish in their homes because their parents spoke in their native tongue and were quite uncomfortable with the English language. Most all dads worked in the copper mines while moms primarily tended to the household. Many of my peers were held back in elementary school due in large part to English language deficiencies. Consequently, my siblings and I were encouraged to speak English exclusively to prepare us for life in a predominantly English speaking nation.

Our childhood past times consisted of outdoor games of kick the can, pick-up games of football or baseball in a makeshift rock strewn field in an arroyo, hikes to the desert hills behind the town or when there was nothing else to do, set up wargames where we divided up into teams of soldiers, built fortifications out of old lumber and tin and piled up rocks as ammunition. One such battle found me at my Aunt's house where she expertly stitched up my head with needle and thread after I fell wounded from an incoming "grenade." We'd also build go carts out of a few old 2X4s and bicycle wheels, using some old rope for steering and a wooden stick as a brake (never worked). The hill our house was sitting on was perfect for the Go cart, we generated great speed and of course the rules of gravity applied and crashes were frequent. My mom finally insisted on us dismantling the cart but not until after many great memories were made. Bicycles were constructed from spare parts pieced together from the local trash dump and worn out inner tubes were "re-purposed" into slingshots, nothing went to waste.

My dad was an early believer in the Boy Scouts of America, so much so that he became the Scoutmaster for the San Pedro Troop as well as the Scoutmaster of our neighboring towns Hayden and Kearny. To this day, when I return to my hometown after over thirty years, I am approached by men who recall fondly their old scoutmaster Mr. Avenetti. I started as a Cub Scout in San Pedro and then as we moved to Hayden I continued along with my three brothers into Boy Scouts with the Troop in Hayden. I'll come back to my Boy Scout experience later, as it was to become a key factor in the establishment of my character foundation and my approach to building young boys into solid young men.

After graduating High School in May of 1980 and like my father before me, I joined the United States Marine Corps at the age of 17. I had no particular reason for joining beyond my perception that Marines were 1st to fight and the fact that they looked great in that uniform didn't hurt. My plan was to serve for four years and then do "something else." Not much of a plan but I simply did not know what I wanted to be or what I wanted to do. What I did know was that I truly wanted to be a Marine. So began my 28 year journey from Private to Chief Warrant Officer 5, a few wars and some shooting matches along the way and more importantly, exposure to some of the best leaders and mentors a young man could hope for.

During these 28 years I was privileged not only to serve my country but also to enjoy some of the best duty assignments a young kid from San Pedro AZ could ever imagine. After all, at 17 years old, as with most 17 year olds, the world was at my feet, I knew it all and had the energy (if not the good sense) to prove it. The Marine Corps would take me to El Salvador in Central America to guard our embassy during that country's civil war, a quick lesson in the fragility of life and the seriousness of our task. As embassy guards we were known as "Ambassadors in Blue" and our role in representing our country was taken very seriously. Because of the violent and dangerous nature of duty in El Salvador I would get my pick of any U.S. embassy, consulate or legation in the world for my 2nd and final duty station. My choice – Geneva Switzerland. In Geneva I would guard the U.S. Mission as well as the Strategic Arms Reduction Talks (START) between the United States and the Soviet Union. I would be privileged to meet then Vice President George H. W. Bush one of the people I respect most in this world along with his wife Barbara, our former 1st Lady who years later as the First Lady, gave me a scolding in the desert of Saudi Arabia for not having a picture of my wife in my wallet. These two great people are American treasures and I absolutely treasure that scolding.

During my tour in Geneva I also took advantage of the geographic convenience of Switzerland and traveled to most of Western Europe and Great Britain. Follow on assignments would find me and my new bride Brenda who I met on recruiting duty in Phoenix Arizona, receive assignments to Hawaii, California, Oklahoma, with additional solo tours in North Carolina and deployments to Okinawa Japan, Korea and combat deployments to Saudi Arabia, Kuwait and Iraq. My most rewarding memories are those from combat deployments where I bore witness to the best of mankind and the worst of mankind, for adversity brings out the best and worst in us and shows our mettle or lack thereof. A tour on recruiting duty would teach me about long hours, human nature, the importance of "listening" as opposed to simply "hearing" and the reward for a job well done. Throughout these years I was fortunate to have great leaders and some who became great mentors, the two are not necessarily mutually inclusive. I could probably write a book on my Marine Corps experiences alone, and it's been suggested that I should but perhaps another time, my passion is in mentoring young boys into strong young men.

A short 28 years after standing on the infamous yellow footprints of Marine Corps Recruit Depot San Diego, CA (I was a Hollywood Marine), I took off my combat boots and hung up my camouflage utility uniform and lay roots in Rockwall, Texas. The Corps had given me lessons in life, loss, service, humility, pride as well as a beautiful bride and three fine young boys now turning into men I am proud to call my sons. As with every Marine who leaves our beloved Corps I would have to figure out who I was supposed to be next. The answer would come in a call to serve once again. After several years as an Assistant Scoutmaster, I was asked to serve our local Boy Scout Troop as the Scoutmaster. I had no significant qualifications beyond having been a Scout myself, reaching the rank of Life Scout, just a step away from Eagle Scout which my older brother Nick would achieve but would regrettably elude me. I had also served as the Troop's Committee Chair, organizing support functions for the troop's operational needs. After contemplation and some persuading from a few Scout Dads I accepted the position and prayed that I would serve capably and to the expectations of the boys and their parents. I have undying respect for those adults who take the time to volunteer their time (our most precious commodity) to mentor our young boys. A common joke among adult Scout leaders is that it only takes an hour per week to volunteer as an adult leader, yes an hour per week… per scout! Let's not even talk about the pay; why last year I asked for and received a 100% pay increase! All joking aside, the reward is in watching these young 11 year old boys enter the Scouting trail and six or seven years later exit that trailhead with heads held high and a true sense of purpose knowing they have been armed with the foundation of values and character that will serve them well in life.

What follows is my attempt to lay out those intangible traits which together may be described as the construct or building blocks of character, that invisible element of collective traits by which we are rightly or wrongly judged. During my years as a leader and mentor to our communities' young Scouts I used my experiences in life and the Marine Corps to impart lessons of character and very often concluded our meetings with a "Scoutmaster's Minute" imparting some wisdom if only in my simple and somewhat narrowly focused way hoping these boys would retain just a few salient points that would sustain them in life's journey. Each Scoutmaster's Minute would have a character trait as the topic such as "Courage, Patriotism, Citizenship, Perseverance, etc." It's funny but by the end of my tenure as Scoutmaster, the boys would begin to bring their parents in for the Scoutmaster's Minute so they too could enjoy my tales of far off places and the exploits of some of America's finest as examples of men of character. As I gave up my position as Scoutmaster, I asked to stay on as the Troop Eagle Scout Advisor, working with the older Scouts in their pursuit of Eagle Scout and continued refinement of their leadership skills and character development. The national average of Scouts who actually achieve the rank of Eagle Scout is around 2%. Our Troop in the last three years is hovering around 30% of our total numbers and rising, and if we view their success as individual scouts who joined our troop and remained for more than 3 years our Eagle stats hover closer to 80%. This is a testament to the determination and focus of these boys and the support of their parents. These boys, along with my own three sons, whom I am immensely proud of, are the reason for this book.

My two youngest sons would achieve Eagle Scout while our eldest son would miss out on the scouting experience largely due to my frequent and prolonged absence for deployments, wars and general duties and obligations to our country and Corps, leaving my lovely wife to juggle the household and children, a job she very capably handled and much credit belongs to her. It has been said of Marine spouses that they have "the toughest job in the Corps," and I for one will not argue this. If we measure our success in life by the legacy we leave behind, then I am exceedingly proud of our boys and very excited for what they will ultimately achieve in life. Well prepared, solid ethical decision making are qualities any father or mother would be very proud of. I have equal affection for the scouts in our troop, especially those I have watched grow into young men and come to know from a "teacher – scholar" perspective as well as from a "father – son" perspective. They have honored me with the opportunity to mentor them, guide them and to be a part of their development.

Throughout this book I will reference Carl Von Clausewitz and his literary masterpiece "On War." The reason I felt this work to be so pertinent to the development of individual character is because the act of war and the genius required to be successful in the conduct of such, pits man against man in a manner no other action or endeavor in life can do. This matching of wills, battle of strategies, and measure of resolve truly digs into the inner strength of character, intellect and fortitude to reveal the prime ingredients of success in life's journey. Von Clausewitz delves into the moral, physical and psychological virtues of the individual as well as the combined factors which come into play in organizational structure, complexity of design, discipline and actions of combat and the strategies involved. If we can elicit even a fraction of the pinnacle traits of the military genius in our boys, we will find a strong young man of character and resolve. Von Clausewitz made the study of war his life's work, and his life truly was a study in war as his first experience in war came as a 12 year old Lance Corporal fighting the French. His compilation of this work was published shortly after his passing by his wife in 1832, need I say more of the strength of the women in our lives?

My other principle source of wisdom comes from my personal experiences with today's foremost military genius, General James N. Mattis whom I was privileged to serve with in combat during Operation Iraqi Freedom and equally important, during the planning phase leading up to combat operations. A student of history and a strategist who has been summoned on several occasions to apply as Von Clausewitz opines the "continuation of policy by other means," we know as "war" on behalf of this great nation. Each time he has come away victorious and in my reflections of his actions, philosophy and intellect I have come to understand the lessons he taught me and how completely relevant they are to the development and nurturing of the young boy into a young man of strength in character and virtue. I offer my experience with the great General as lessons in manhood as few could be a better example of what we would hope our young boys to become.

This combination of knowledge, wisdom and experience I offer in the following work in the hope that it may bring some insight, create some spark of light, and expose some ideals which may be of value in your commitment to building your boy into a young man. Most likely you will not see imme-diate results, not to worry, your boys will gradually grow their value system almost imperceptibly and one day you'll find yourself watching them with a smile on your face because they have finally got it. This journey you are tak-ing along with your boy is a privilege, a gift earned in your own life's journey and a gift you must pass on to your sons. I wish you the joy and fulfillment with your boys that I have been blessed with in raising my boys and helping mentor my scouts. Enjoy the trail!

CHAPTER 2

ON COURAGE

I begin with courage because courage lays the foundation for all other traits and actions; it is the basis for good and ethical choice, for difficult and challenging action and of course the basis for inaction in its absence. Courage is both physical and moral where it has been said that moral courage is more important than physical courage, subjective of course but seemingly always true in the greater construct of character. We can see examples of both throughout our history and in many instances we look beyond the moral courage and only see the physical courage. Moral courage, the strength of character to act in a way which is counterintuitive based on human instinct for self-preservation, in other words while everyone else is going left to avoid the difficult road, you go right because you know the bumps along the difficult road carry lessons too important to pass up for the smooth and easy road. While physical courage may be displayed by the Infantryman who charges a machine gun nest because his buddies are being killed and wounded, or the policemen and first responders who ran towards the towering infernos of the twin towers immediately after they were destroyed in a cowardly act of terror on 11 September, 2001. It may be argued that the act of physical courage may be precipitated by moral courage, the decision to act in such a dangerous manner, this may be explained by training and muscle memory, and we'll discuss this aspect later in the book.

As with anything in life and with respect to character there is a counterbalance and courage is no different, were we to have undaunted courage or recklessness, we would die a fools death a thousand times over. So, we temper courage with prudence, with analysis, with probability to calculate the proper balance between courage and recklessness. If we are successful in developing a young man of character we must first build in them the trait of courage because courage is the precursor to all other action and all other virtues. This entry argument of courage formulates the basis for integrity, moral strength, initiative, decisiveness and all other important factors in our individual value system. When taken in conjunction with action, courage breeds our political leaders, entrepreneurs, military leaders and first responders to name a few.

During combat operations in Iraq a young Marine Sergeant involved in a firefight with enemy forces would, along with his comrades, fall wounded by enemy fire. In their fight to fend off the onslaught of enemy insurgents during the fight, a grenade would land in their midst and next to the Sergeant. Whether instinctively or through involuntary muscle reflex the Sergeant pulled the grenade beneath him and absorbed the full force of the blast. Without going into the deliberation of whether or not the Sergeant made a conscious decision or whether it was reflexive, there is no doubt this act in and of itself was physically courageous. The knowing or willing sacrifice of one's life for the benefit of his brothers with complete disregard for his own safety. I would argue that the Sergeant had no intuitive muscle memory or training to cause this action rather, he demonstrated moral courage in reaching for that grenade and physical courage in the act itself.

We need look no further than our nation's struggle for civil rights and the actions of Rosa Parks for an example of moral courage. Not only a black but also a female in an era of racial segregation and prejudice, Ms. Rosa Parks would demonstrate the moral fiber and strength of character we define as moral courage and set an example for an entire race and generations to come to emulate. Ms. Parks could have waited for someone else to act yet she knowingly and calculatingly understood the predicament and potential dangers of her actions when she refused to surrender her seat to a white passenger on that bus in Montgomery, Alabama. If we were to examine the event more closely we could extrapolate many lessons, good and bad, where strength of character was present and no doubt where strength of character was glaringly absent. Understanding the culture in those days, what would you have done had you been a passenger in that bus? What would your son have done? Courage must be paired with action or it is simply a thought, a thought as meaningless as if you thought of the ability to fly, or to bring world peace; no action, no result.

A personal account. Having served in combat under perhaps the greatest military mind of our era, General James N. Mattis; I can offer assessment of the element of courage from personal perspective. General Mattis while commanding the 1st Marine Division understood with perfect clarity the importance and the distinction between moral and physical courage as they relate to warfare. His every action sought to bolster the moral purity of purpose our division of Marines were about to face in the form of combat. He completely understood that the strength and resolve of the division, the moral fiber, would prove an overwhelming ally in the execution of warfare. Notes author Carl Von Clausewitz in his seminal publication "On War" as he opines at length as to this intangible inanimate feature of individual and collective character which so heavily weighs the odds of victory in battle; "History provides the strongest proof of the importance of moral factors and their often incredible effect: this is the noblest and most solid nourishment that the mind of a general may draw from a study of the past." For those who follow or have studied General Mattis, they will know that he is an avid student of history and his personal library numbers well over 6,000 books by many accounts. His actions in preparation for the historical attack from Kuwait into Iraq and on to Baghdad were calculated and studied with respect to the generation of the moral fiber of his division. I offer a copy of the letter then Major General Mattis penned and ordered delivered to each of the over 20,000 warriors of the 1st Marine Division before we crossed the Line of Departure into battle.

March 2003

1ˢᵗ Marine Division (REIN)

Commanding General's Message to All Hands

For decades, Saddam Hussein has tortured, imprisoned, raped and murdered the Iraqi people; invaded neighboring countries without provocation; and threatened the world with weapons of mass destruction. The time has come to end his reign of terror. On your young shoulders rest the hopes of mankind.

When I give you the word, together we will cross the Line of Departure, close with those forces that choose to fight, and destroy them. Our fight is not with the Iraqi people, nor is it with members of the Iraqi army who choose to surrender. While we will move swiftly and aggressively against those who resist, we will treat all others with decency, demonstrating chivalry and soldierly compassion for people who have endured a lifetime under Saddam's oppression.

Chemical attack, treachery, and use of the innocent as human shields can be expected, as can other unethical tactics. Take it all in stride. Be the hunter, not the hunted: never allow your unit to be caught with its guard down. Use good judgement and act in best interests of our Nation.

You are part of the world's most feared and trusted force. Engage your brain before you engage your weapon. Share your courage with each other as we enter the uncertain terrain north of the Line of Departure. Keep faith in your comrades on your left and right and Marine Air overhead. Fight with a happy heart and strong spirit.

For the mission's sake, our country's sake, and the sake of the men who carried the Division's colors in past battles-*who fought for life and never lost their nerve*-carry out your mission and *keep your honor clean*. Demonstrate to the world there is "No Better Friend, No Worse Enemy" than a U.S. Marine.

J.N. Mattis
Major General, U.S. Marines
Commanding

Take your boys to a local veteran's organization so they can meet some of our humble heroes, you may be surprised at some of the stories they can tell about courage, both physical and moral. Ideally have them read some short excerpts of historical battles before they visit. Many of these veterans can no longer walk, some from wounds suffered in America's battles, some simply from old age. Have your boys introduce themselves, look the veteran in the eye and tell them why they are there, your boy will have immediate respect and maybe some pretty cool stories to pass on to his buddies. I belong to a unique group of veterans here in Rockwall that meets each Friday for comradeship and laughter, we have been given the name "My Band of Brothers," by former U.S. Congressman Ralph Hall, the oldest American ever to serve actively in the U. S. House of Representatives. One Friday, Congressman Hall himself a veteran of World War II as a fighter pilot in the Navy, invited a special guest and personal friend of his to join us. To our surprise it was none other than the last man to walk on the moon, astronaut and retired Navy Captain Gene Cernan. I brought my then 17 year old son and Eagle Scout, Gunner to come and meet Capt. Cernan, a true legend, hero and great American man of courage. Imagine the courage not only to fly into space but to actually step out of that capsule and walk on the moon. This is a memory Gunner now serving in the United States Air Force, cherishes to this day. *Gene Cernan has passed since the writing of this book, I will always cherish meeting this great American and having known "The Congressman."

Your boy may consider himself void of courage and this is okay, most teens and pre-teens haven't sufficiently challenged themselves nor has life challenged them to the extent that they may gauge their caliber of courage. Many men will go to their grave not knowing what the limits of their courage might have been. Don't despair, when they are introduced to models of courage, they will understand the extent to which some men will go and have gone in the demonstration of moral and physical courage whether by necessity or by choice. Take them out to a zip line course, a rappelling tower, or a local rock climb. Very often they will learn about facing their fear and perhaps a small measure of their physical courage. Don't discourage them or admonish them if they fail, rather introduce them to small steps in addressing courage. I have known many brave Marines who have an absolute visceral fear of heights but one look at the medals on their chest will tell you a different story of their courage. They won't know what they are afraid of until they are faced with it. Remember, you may not see the fruits of your efforts until they are older and faced with decisions, choices or actions which demand courage, you are laying the foundation for these choices and it is equally important as the act itself.

CHAPTER 3

ON INTEGRITY

M y father would say that integrity is merely doing the right thing, especially when no one is watching. If we assess the meaning of integrity we may say that integrity is being whole, complete and without weakness. Its Latin origin comes from the Roman Centurions who would proclaim their armor as "integritas" or without flaw when being inspected for battle. The soldier being inspected would pound his armor with his fist and shout "integritas." In comparison, the Roman Praetorian Guards (imperial body guards) would shout "Hail Caesar" signifying their allegiance was to Caesar, not to their legion. It is important to observe that this seemingly minor act would signal the fracture of the warrior code of ideals and the breakdown of discipline. Once the mindset shifts from loyalty to the greater nation, organization or team to loyalty to a man, the wholeness or strength of the team weakens. This character trait is critical to ethical decision making as well as accountability for one's actions.

The Marine Corps lists Integrity as one of the 14 traits of a good leader. A leader will find themselves under a magnifying glass, someone always looking at your every action or inaction and often passing judgment. Good, bad or indifferent, this is human nature and when done in an objective manner, it is useful in assessing the performance and/or advancement prospects of a current or future leader. Integrity speaks to the core strength of the body, or in this case, the boy. Remember, there is no right way to do the wrong thing. I offer for review the 14 Leadership Traits of the United States Marine. Some are included in this book while others will not be included for various reasons however, all 14 traits will be touched upon in some manner throughout.

Justice	Judgment
Dependability	Integrity
Decisiveness	Tact
Initiative	Enthusiasm
Bearing	Unselfishness
Courage	Knowledge
Loyalty	Endurance

While growing up in Arizona in the late 60's and 70's we would travel to Tucson on payday to buy groceries and if we were lucky hit the McDonalds or a movie (we had neither in our town). On one particular trip, we came out of the grocery store to find a woman standing at our car with her children. The lady, a minority and obviously not of any sort of financial means to speak of had run into our car with her car and damaged the fender. My father immediately saw this as a teaching point and kindly thanked the lady for having the integrity to wait for us and confess her guilt for the accident when she clearly could have driven off and likely gotten away with the infraction. He forgave her the incident and any related cost for repairs knowing such a bill would surely set her back where she clearly could use the money to feed and care for her family. Had my Father demanded compensation the message to her children as well as me and my siblings may have been mixed and given doubt to the benefit of integrity. No doubt that lady paid it forward and used this as a teaching point for her children. The reward for acts of integrity only serve to bolster this foundational character trait and we as adults carry this responsibility of setting the example.

In a broader example we need look no further than political figures who while entrusted with the common good of our democratic republic have on several occasions betrayed that trust by flaws in their moral armor, cracks in their shield of truth and trust. We are called to trust our elected officials because by virtue of our right to vote we have put them on a pedestal for all to see and emulate, proclaiming ethical behavior, moral conduct, truth and fidelity to our constitution and we rightfully hold them to this high standard.

Yet examples of infidelity, fraud, lies and greed seem to be widespread. It is so disappointing to hear about violations of trust between political figures and their constituents or worse yet violations of the law, all the while it seems that they receive a pass whereas, if we had committed a similar infraction we would find ourselves behind bars. We have become accustomed to hearing "Well that's politics." and this cannot continue or we will have abandoned the moral high ground for the convenience of a "boys will be boys" mentality. The truth and trust we place in our elected officials at all levels must maintain the integrity of the centurion's armor lest the shield protecting this great experiment of democracy shatter. We need look no further than our history books for examples of failed states and in many instances, the failure can be traced back to weakness of character in their leaders.

Not only can we site failed states, the books are littered with failed corporations whose leadership abandoned their integrity and their stakeholders in the name of greed. The shocking self-destruction of Enron at the hands of Kenneth Lay and his team of corporate big wigs destroyed the wealth of multitudes of investors who placed their trust in him. His overt lack of integrity and any semblance of sound ethics resulted in the fall of Enron and numerous related corporate firms such as Arthur Andersen an auditing firm. Bernie Madoff brought the term "Ponzi scheme" to our dinner tables and destroyed the wealth of all who placed their trust in him through a series of good money after bad investment schemes which deceived investors and lined his pockets. There are simply too many examples of failure of integrity to even attempt to mention them. Suffice it to say that integrity must guide our decision making process because the minute we abandon our integrity, we take our first step into the abyss of iniquity and expose ourselves to the fate of those nefarious characters who went before us.

As we analyze integrity as a byproduct of the moral foundation of courage, we can easily see where integrity also supports additional traits such as honesty, hard work, unselfishness etc. We can look at our value system as sort of a pyramid with courage as the roots system, or the base of the pyramid and all other virtues as offshoots from the base.

Show your boys the meaning of integrity first by setting an example for him to emulate, especially in the most difficult situations. Discourage lies in favor of self-accountability, this should not be in a harsh manner unless there is safety or harm involved rather, it should be in the form of a lesson about truth and trust. Once we abandon our moral high ground, it is very difficult to win it back. I encourage my boys, when tempted to place blame for a mistake or failure to look in the mirror first and make an honest assessment as to who is really at fault. I have learned to cut them off at the first sign of "But it wasn't my fau..." Make it a practice, even when it is obvious they are not at fault, this will build their critical thinking skills as well as integrity. Discuss issues in the daily news which point to ready lessons in integrity or lack thereof. Remind them of historical figures who fell from grace because of greed, ego and malfeasance, all flaws in integrity and what could have been done to prevent such events. Integrity is a habit, practice it like shooting hoops or making your bed, once it becomes a habit, you are less likely to stray from it.

CHAPTER 4

ON HUMOR

I grew up watching some of the old classic sitcoms and variety shows as well as some of the most talented actors and actresses in our recent history such as Carol Burnett, Tim Conway, Jackie Gleeson, Art Carney and Jerry Lewis to name a few. These talented people had the extraordinary talent of making people laugh and as the old saying goes "laughter is the best medicine." As we analyze the many traits of character we cannot underestimate the value of having a sense of humor. Not necessarily laughing at other's jokes or comics rather, it should begin with being able to laugh at yourself. We can't take ourselves so seriously that we fail to see the humor in our mistakes, our weaknesses or our overt and often failing attempts at humor. Conversely, any opportunity to put a smile on someone's face should be happily pursued. Life has a way of tearing the smile off our face, failing a test, money worries, losing a job, relationship break-up or even a death. We have a choice in how we deal with this, and we'll talk more about "Choice" later.

Too often we hear of comedians who claim fame for making fun of others, often in a condescending way. It seems almost as if this is the new form of humor, laughter at other people's expense rather than the old days where the comedian made you laugh at him/her. Don Rickles famously had a reputation for insulting people but he did it to their face and in a manner that typically had the target laughing harder than the audience. Surely there is occasion to have a good laugh at other's expense however, when we establish this as the norm, we have lost sight of the value and importance of self-deprecating humor and humor in general. This type of self-deprecating humor hurts no one and has the tangential effect of building our own inner strength and emotional body armor, traits very important in this age of growing social media and finger-tip communication.

During Operation Desert Shield and Desert Storm I was serving in a Marine artillery battery, the big guns also known as "The King of Battle" were arrayed in battle ready positions along the Saudi desert border with Kuwait, far removed from civilization and any semblance of household amenities. Daily tasks included digging fighting positions and the most dreaded of all was being assigned to burn the barrels of excrement each morning. I'll defer on the latter topic and relate an occurrence one particularly hot afternoon when one of our Marines we'll call Smitty was assigned "extra" duties of digging a particularly deep fighting hole, so deep in fact that Smitty who was about 6 feet 4 inches tall had to be helped out of the hole with a rope. Now Smitty it seemed was always in some sort of trouble, and to his credit he always happily accepted his sentence with a shake of the head and a smile as if to say, "you caught me." As luck would have it, our Commanding General was paying us a visit that day and he happened to walk by the hole and looked in to see where all the dirt was flying out from. He said "Good afternoon Marine, look like you can use some help down there." Without missing a beat, Smitty handed his shovel up to the General. Now our 1stSgt had a look of horror on his face but the General immediately found an opportunity for humor and said, "Oh, I didn't mean me!" Later, we all had a good laugh including Smitty, and he found himself digging a whole new hole the next day.

Years later in 2002 while assigned to the Planning Cell of 1st Marine Division, forward deployed to Kuwait with the mission of planning the initial invasion of Iraq known as Operation Iraqi Freedom. One day, our higher headquarters contacted me, knowing I had served previous tours in Kuwait, they asked if I had ever been out to Bubiyan Island. I replied that I had a few years earlier during Operation Desert Thunder. Now Bubiyan is located at the head of the Persian Gulf between Iraq and Kuwait and Iraq has long claimed Bubiyan as its own. The Brits I was informed, would soon be arriving in Kuwait and the Artillery Brigadier wanted to conduct a reconnaissance of Bubiyan for potential artillery positions to provide fire support for their upcoming amphibious operations. I agreed to escort the Brigadier to Bubiyan. Well, the day of my mission I was readying my security force when

General Mattis, Commanding General of 1st Marine Division came walking up and he had his eye on me. "Avenetti" he yelled. "Yes Sir?" I replied. "I hear you are taking the Brits out to Bubiyan." "Yes Sir" I said. "Do you have enough security?" he asked, "Yes Sir." Do you have enough weapons and ammunition?" "Yes Sir." Then he leaned in and said "Don't you get captured you understand me." I said "Yes Sir, I won't get captured." He leaned in a little closer with the look only those closest to the great General knew and said, "I mean it, don't you get captured, you know too much." You see I was the Targeting Officer for the division and I had selected, prioritized and pre-planned all the targets for the upcoming battle. I replied, "No Sir, I won't get captured, if they capture me, I'll kill myself." To which the General replied, "No, don't kill yourself, just wound yourself and crawl back, I'll kill you." You see, even the General had a sense of humor... I hope. By the way, my time working for General Mattis is my most cherished experience in leadership. His methods, his thought process, his ability to analyze and decide is beyond profound, it is quite simply, brilliant.

Encourage your boys to smile and laugh, and most of all to laugh at themselves. Life is serious enough, take the time to seek out humorous events or even a good joke and most importantly to try and make other people laugh, even at your expense. Don't take yourself too seriously, really we aren't so important that we can't deal with some self-deprecating humor, believe me, there will be plenty of time for seriousness throughout their lives. This is a learned trait and the best way to teach them is by setting the example. You may not be the type prone to humor and if you are like me, terrible at telling jokes, (I have two, maybe three "Go to" jokes in my repertoire) but there are other ways to lighten up a crowd. Be willing to take a pie to the face so to speak, which never gets old. Next time you have a chance to watch a little television with your boy, turn it to a channel that show some of the old classic sitcoms. He may think it's corny at first but I guarantee you'll see a smile before long and it will definitely generate discussion about that funny looking thing sitting on a hook that's referred to as a telephone. Imagine being tethered to a wall just to hold a conversation, and how does one send a text over that contraption, and while we're at it, how come everything is in black and white?

CHAPTER 5

ON SITUATIONAL AWARENESS

N ow more than ever before we see our boys walking around with their face buried in a phone, headsets plugged into their ears and a sense that anything that matters is all contained in that wonderful device they hold in their hands and the information flow streaming to their ears in stereo or the latest text or video for their viewing pleasure. Meanwhile the world spins on, vehicles drive by, a bird flies overhead, a weather front approaches and a mugging happens a mere twenty feet away yet little Johnnie ambles on seemingly impervious to anything this wonderful world could possibly throw at him until that light pole somehow leaps right in front of him and crash! Seriously, this is only a slight exaggeration, look in the rear view mirror next time you are driving them somewhere and guaranteed, they aren't paying attention to the road or to your driving skills, rather they are buried in their phone killing zombies or crushing candies. Now far be it for me to outlaw candy crushing or zombie killing but when we close off two if not three of our senses, we simply do not have situational awareness and this is potentially very dangerous.

I've preached to my boys their whole lives about the importance of situational awareness yet somehow I don't think they truly comprehend the potential impact for disregarding this. Somehow I think they just figure it's just Dad with another one of his "this is really important" life stories. We can idly say "well that's just how teenagers are," but my experience with teenagers in combat is that this is not necessarily true. I have known young

Marines learn to use and trust their senses because it may mean the difference between life and death. It would be easy to excuse the lackadaisical behavior of our boys if it were not for the fact they are allowed to control (or not) a 2 ton 400 horsepower hunk of metal (and some fiberglass) flying down the road at 60 plus miles per hour. Situational awareness, you better believe it is very important.

My Marine Corps leaders have for decades pounded the importance of situational awareness into me and my peers and no doubt they have been doing this for generations because the quickest way to come home in a metal box or on a stretcher is by not keeping one's head in the ballgame. As General James N. Mattis was fond of saying; "the most important six inches on the battlefield is between your ears." The great general invoked a "Guardian Angel" policy within the 1st Marine Division, this policy simply ensured that wherever Marines were there would always be dedicated Marines on security watch, they would be termed "Guardian Angels." I know many General Mattis quotes because I was privileged to hear many of them first hand. We need look no further for an example of manhood and leadership than General Mattis and much of what I learned comes from his example and leadership.

Just after the cessation of hostilities in Desert Storm as a young Gunnery Sergeant, I was driving a High Mobility Multi-Wheeled Vehicle (commonly referred to as a Hummer) with a few Marine buddies of mine. We were quite honestly touring the battlefield mostly out of curiosity and maybe some war trophies when one of my buddies hollered "Stop!" Looking to our left and right we could see the distinct and uniform humps of landmines just underneath the surface of the desert sand. We were in fact in the middle of a minefield! Well, you never saw a Hummer move in a more precise manner in reverse right back out along its original tracks than we did that day. A funny story to tell years later but the potential consequences were absolute life or death, the elation of victory brings about a haze if we are not mentally attentive... situational awareness - absent.

At 1:30 PM on 3 May 2015, my good friend police Sergeant Greg Stevens reported for a voluntary extra duty assignment at the Curtis Culwell Center in Dallas, TX where there was to be a controversial art contest called "Draw the Prophet." Stevens's assignment, to guard the west parking lot entrance and allow only designated personnel access. Taking account of his area of responsibility he placed traffic cones to better control access and positioned himself in the opening. Stevens was also joined by a Garland I.S.D. security officer who was in uniform but unarmed. So began what was a fairly typical day, vetting vehicles and preventing unauthorized access.

At approximately 6:50 PM, roughly 5 hours into what was a routine shift a small black 2 door vehicle abruptly pulled partially into the driveway parallel to the street and came to a stop. Officer Stevens was alerted by the manner in which the vehicle came to a stop, something wasn't right. He shifted his focus to the black car noticing it had out of state plates (Arizona) and suddenly both driver and passenger doors opened and the occupants started to get out. As Officer Stevens noticed the barrel of a long gun come up he immediately drew his police issued pistol, a Glock 21 (.45 caliber) and exchanged gunfire with the first assailant until he fell to the ground wounded. Stevens immediately acquired the second assailant (the driver) who was also armed with a long gun and had made his way to the back of the vehicle. This second assailant was firing on the other security officer who was attempting to move to cover as he did not have a weapon to engage the attacker. Stevens fires several more rounds from his Glock and the driver then falls wounded. The officer of over 30 years' experience instinctively turns back to the passenger who although wounded still posed a threat. He engaged him again until he believed the threat to be neutralized and then returned to reengage the driver and fired on him again until he believed this threat neutralized as well. Stevens immediately executed a tactical reload and moved toward the first attacker who was mortally wounded but still moving around when backup arrived on the scene.

Imagine the carnage had Officer Stevens not had the situational awareness, presence of mind and tactical training to say nothing of courage to address this grave and deadly threat. What if there had been improvised explosive devices either on their person or aboard the vehicle? The consequences in this case were absolutely dire and a potential mass casualty event was thwarted because one man saw, sensed and acted. What would you do given similar circumstances? Would you have possessed the mettle, the instantaneous decision making cycle and the skills to act so courageously, so boldly? Most would not but thankfully Officer Stevens did and countless people are alive today because of his actions.

Teach your boys to pay attention to their surroundings, be aware in crowded areas, malls, stadiums and anywhere people gather in large numbers because the reality of the world we now live in is; regardless of our views, there are bad actors out there trying to kill us. They only have to be lucky once, we must be diligent always. Encourage them to take the headphones out and listen to their surroundings, take their eyes off the mobile phone and take in the area, visually scanning for things out of place, or maybe just enjoying the scenery. Have them learn street signs, and various routes to school. Ask them to tell you three things they observed while riding to school or to church.

While on Embassy duty in the 1980's way before the years of persistent terror threats we were taught to vary our routes, never create a pattern and always be aware of our surroundings. You see, even in the 1980's the threat of terror was alive and well for Americans serving overseas. When in a public area such as a restaurant, always seek to place your back to a surface and your field of view to as many entry points as possible, visually scanning the area at frequent intervals for anything out of place or suspicious actions. All it takes for bad things to happen is for good people to do nothing, and if you see or hear nothing, you will do nothing. Take a hunter's mentality, be the lion, not the sheep, this is not an aggressive stance, it is a heightened state of awareness.

Recently while out with my wife, we walked into a local establishment for lunch. As usual, I quickly scanned the establishment and asked the hostess for a specific table providing me with a good vantage point of the whole room. Being a gentleman, my wife is always seated first but she knows my tactics and selects a seat with her back to the entrance. Shortly after placing our order, I leaned over to her and said "take a look around the room, do you notice anything odd?" She didn't quite know where I was going with this so she replied, "No, what's going on?" I said, "Look at every male guest in this place, they all have their backs to the entrance." They have lost any advantage of situational awareness should something go awry. Some may say this is paranoid, I would counter that the sheep that doesn't see the lion approaching is typically the first one served for dinner. A man looks out for the safety and wellbeing of his family.

Train your boys by first setting an example of good behaviors in situational awareness. Be observant, watching and listening whenever you leave your safe environment. Next time you go to a restaurant to eat, a concert or public event, make sure you are facing the entrance or at least a majority of the dining/gathering area. This is a passive security posture, trust me, no one will have a clue what you are up to and it just may pay off one day. Know where the entrance and exits are and have a mental contingency plan. Explain to your boys the importance of watching for things out of the norm and what to do if danger is approaching. It is too easy to let our guard down but in today's terrorism filled world, we have a responsibility to be diligent and watch out for each other. You won't always have an Officer Stevens watching over you, you must be the guardian angel of your family.

CHAPTER 6

ON RESPECT

O ur teens today are faced with several definitions of respect, so much so that it seems they may not really know or appreciate what respect truly is. Respect must begin in the mirror, if we don't respect ourselves then we can't understand what it means to respect someone else or perhaps a cause or ideal. When we were young we were taught to respect our elders, respect our teachers and respect those people in positions of authority such as police officers. Yet today we see more than ever the seeming carnage of attacks and targeting of our officers of the law – no respect. It seems our youth confuse respect with fame where they follow and sometimes emulate and idolize the every move of pop stars, movie stars or athletes through social media because it is so important to know what they had for lunch, if their coffee was too hot or their designer jeans fit just right. In the midst of this we must maintain our moral compass and instill in our teens the understanding of how important it is to respect ourselves, our mind, our bodies and our spirit. Once self-respect is recognized through establishing personal values, we move on to respecting others. Having said this, we must also impart on our teens the need to discern between those who should be respected and those who demand respect. Respect must be earned, by you and by those who seek your respect.

There is an old tale of a legendary Marine General by the name of Lewis B. "Chesty" Puller who when coming across a young Lieutenant standing in front of a Private who was performing multiple salutes to the young Officer.

Chesty asked the Lieutenant what was going on and the Lieutenant replied "This Marine failed to salute me and I am teaching him a lesson in respect." To which Chesty replied "It would occur to me that each of these salutes from the young Private deserves a salute in return from you as well, you've got some catching up to do Lieutenant." The lesson here is that position or rank alone does not automatically assign you respect, it may assign you authority but respect must be earned. In the military a subordinate must respect the "rank" of a superior but respect for the individual must be earned through time and action, it is not automatic. Similarly in the workplace where the boss has authority, he/she does not automatically have respect, they must earn it. Remember, respect is owned by the servant and bestowed upon the leader, likewise, it may be revoked by the servant. The leader must constantly earn respect through hard work, leading by example, moral actions and ethical decisions.

We must also ensure that our boys understand that respect is not equal to entitlement. A leader must always place the needs of their team ahead of their own because the success of the team is infinitely more important than the accolades for the leader. While an organization may accord their leader some privileges, the leader who flaunts these privileges in the face of their subordinates will quickly lose the respect of their team. A Colonel on the Division staff was in a hurry to grab chow and get back to work so he headed to the mess hall and placed himself at the head of the chow line, cutting off several Marines who had been waiting in line. It just so happened that the Colonel did not realize that the last person in line was the Commanding General. The General walked up to the Colonel and asked him if he was in a hurry, and if he believed his time was any more important than these young Marines he just bypassed. Needless to say the Colonel quickly saw the error in his ways and moved most directly to the end of the line. The Colonel lost respect that day, something tells me this Colonel never really earned respect at any time in his career, while respect for the General rose to new heights in the eyes of his Marines.

Remind your boys that respect starts in the mirror and that earning respect can only be bestowed upon them by others, never demanded. They should respect their body by providing it with good nourishment and regular exercise. I don't judge those who choose to decorate their bodies with tattoos however, one way I choose to respect my body is to keep it void of all markings not bestowed upon it by our creator. Nourish the mind with reading and intellectual curiosity, research and investigate, not only will this nourish the mind, it will also educate on history. Nourish the soul with daily prayer and exercise in faith. Remind them that respect must be re-earned daily and if lost, will be very difficult to win back, if ever at all. Remind them that respect is earned by one's actions and by one's words, and to be mindful of how they address others and how they comport themselves, someone is always watching. Social media can be an incubator for disrespect, and what they write or text and submit to social media or even email can never be withdrawn; that egg cannot be unscrambled. Apply the golden rule; "Do unto others as you would have them do unto you."

It seems that people feel much more comfortable commenting or posting hurtful comments online instead of standing face to face to deal with them, this is also a form of disrespect as well as cowardice. Cyber-bullying, is bullying and shows a complete lack of respect. Teach your boys empathy, it is an acquired trait which can be nurtured over time; the ability to understand what others feel and deal with them in a compassionate manner. It has been my observation that bullying is cowardice in the purest form and a level of empathy should be exercised before "posting" something to the internet which could be hurtful or misinterpreted as mean spirited. Yes, even a Marine can have compassion… but it should never be mistaken for weakness.

CHAPTER 7

ON PERSEVERANCE

Have you ever run across a young boy that is too quick to quit at something because they are "tired" or because it's "too hard?" Welcome to the club, teens have to be taught work ethic and perseverance, in other words, quit and failure should have no place in their day to day lexicon. This is not to say that failure will not happen rather, failure should not be a part of their original plan, nor should it be an acceptable option. Failure should be the result only when all available resources have been expended and they have given the task their absolute best. I tell my teens, "You have to earn tired." My father would tell me "You're too young to be tired" and this truly sums up the situation, whether it is a physically exerting task or a mentally taxing problem, giving up is simply not an option. We'll talk more about the attributes of failure later.

In the summer of 2010 my Mother was diagnosed with stage 4 uterine cancer, she was told there was nothing that could be done and that she should go home, get her affairs in order and try to live out her remaining days as comfortable as possible. Now my Mother raised five kids, four boys and one girl, all of whom served in the military, she sent three of her children off to combat for a total of over 72 months. She watched her husband and our Father die in her lap of a massive heart attack on the way to the hospital. She had been diagnosed at the age of 55 with Severe Chronic Inflammatory Demyelinating Polyneuropathy and told that she would likely never walk again, yet she put CIDP in its place and within a year was walking 2 miles daily until her final months. She was not about to take "you're done" for an answer. After being diagnosed with cancer, she vowed to fight and not accept the doctor's prognosis. Five and a half years, major surgeries, chemotherapy and radiation treatments later she would finally succumb to the disease, but not without a fight and some extraordinary life lessons for all who were privileged to spend time with her.

Here is what she taught us along the way. She taught us that life is brittle, but it becomes more brittle the less we maintain it. My Mother would go for a walk every day just as soon as the blazing Arizona sun would dip low enough to provide a bit of shade and some relief from the desert heat. She would put on her sneakers, grab a bottle of water and her walking stick (for the wayward wild desert boars or dogs) and hit the road with purpose. My siblings and I would take every opportunity to walk along her side whenever we could. She would keep this up until very late in her fight when she was simply too weak to even stand without effort. Her strength of faith was incredible, she would attend church regularly and pray daily. She taught us that we must possess a thirst for life; that travel and adventure are not only for the affluent, she travelled every chance she got to places like Italy, Germany, Mexico City, Hawaii as well as many of the contiguous United States. Most important of all; she taught us of the importance of family; that family is the only constant we have, to join in times of celebration and to be relied upon in times of need. She fought to the end and taught us all what perseverance is. Look, giving up is easy, if we want something of worth in our lives we need to be prepared to work for it, this includes life itself.

On June 15, 1966 Marine Staff Sergeant Jimmie Howard, already a veteran and hero of the Korean War and father of six would find himself back in combat in Vietnam and in charge of a 17 man (15 Marines and 2 Navy Corpsmen) Reconnaissance Team heli-lifted to the top of Hill 488 in the middle of enemy territory. After two days of calling in artillery and close air support, the situation was beginning to turn bad but Howard requested to remain on the hill for another day and continue to direct fire on the enemy. By the time higher headquarters confirmed that 200 – 250 enemy soldiers were moving on Hill 488 it was too late to pull Howard and his men off the hill. The enemy struck that night, assaulting Howard's and his men's position from every direction with automatic weapons, grenades and heavy guns. The attacks came all night long, one wave after another, Howard would move amongst his men bolstering their morale and encouraging them to hang in there and fight. Howard's indomitable spirit would sustain his men throughout the night. When the enemy launched another attack Howard and his men began to laugh at them. The enemy was caught off guard and the attack stopped. Surely the enemy was mesmerized, how could these men be laughing? Running low on ammunition, Howard ordered his men to throw rocks at the charging enemy and laugh at them as if they were unconcerned at their perilous situation. At times the fighting was hand-to-hand and Howard would direct close air support strafing runs to within 30 feet of his own position.

By morning's light the now wounded Howard continued to encourage his men to hang in there, motivating them as only a combat veteran leader of his experience could; help was on the way he told them. Meantime a rescue helicopter was shot down while trying to land on the battered hilltop, radio batteries were all dead or destroyed and higher headquarters fearing the worst, sent an entire company of Marines to recover the remains of Howard's unit. By noon the rescue effort reached the hilltop and found five Marines dead, (one more would die on the way to the aid station), 12 wounded and among the 12 wounded there remained only 8 rounds of ammunition.

Gunnery Sergeant Howard would be awarded the Medal of Honor, in addition, his men would receive; 4 Navy Crosses (Our nation's 2nd highest award for valor), 13 Silver Stars (Our nation's 3rd highest award for valor) and 18 Purple Hearts, every man on that hilltop was killed or wounded – perseverance.

I take extra time with Perseverance because the indomitable American spirit must remain a centerpiece of our value system if we are to pass on a country as strong or stronger than we have enjoyed and a country which we know will continue to thrive in an ever increasingly competitive world. Our World War II veterans also known as the "Greatest Generation" came back to a grateful nation after years of fighting, they had the GI Bill, earned their degrees and helped build the country we know today. Our boys are all too often taught that it is okay to give up, that participation is the goal not victory. They are all awarded with certificates for participation, and patted on the back for trying when trying is truly subjective. Did they merely try or did they give it their all? My boys catch themselves beginning to say "I am tired" but always stop short remembering my "tiring" lectures on what "tired" really is. Take your boys to a children's hospital or the oncology ward, or worse yet, to a children's oncology ward and they will see what true perseverance is. Tell them about the Bataan Death March, or the Prisoners of War in the Hanoi Hilton in Vietnam, I am sure you can find a YouTube video or documentary on line, and the next time they say, "I am tired." Remind them what tired really is.

On this topic I would be remiss if I did not mention the indomitable spirit and perseverance of today's fighting force. Having been in battle for over 16 years, some of whom joined immediately after 9/11 like my nephew who joined the Marine Corps and has only known a wartime military. He has had more combat deployments and more cumulative time in combat than anyone I have ever met, and yet he continues to serve. Quitting in a foot race means you don't get a ribbon or medal, quitting a job means you don't get a pay check, quitting in battle means you die. The more we practice quitting, the more we become comfortable with the option. Americans don't quit, a man does not quit on his family, quitting is simply not an option.

CHAPTER 8

ON SELFLESSNESS

We can define selflessness as doing something for others while expecting nothing in return. This trait is often overlooked as simply being kind or considerate while in truth it can and should be something much more significant. In a "what's in it for me society" where self-gratification and personal needs often trump the needs of the under-privileged we too often see our teens opting for a selfie with a celebrity instead of a food drive for the needy. For this essential trait of a leader I offer three stories as examples.

While on one of our trips to Tucson with my Father in the mid-1970s to buy school clothes, we were walking through the department store when a lady who happened to be shopping nearby us, suddenly stiffened, fell straight back to the floor and began convulsing wildly. My father immediately recognized this for what it was, an epileptic seizure. He swiftly moved to assist the lady by inserting his hand in her mouth to keep her from biting or swallowing her tongue. When the lady finally calmed down and help began to show up, my father calmly got up and began to walk away, summoning us to follow him. Shortly thereafter, a store employee ran up to us asking if we knew who it was that helped the lady. My Mother was about to say something when my father said, "sorry we don't know anything about it." The employee said, "Someone said it was you Sir." My father responded "No, they must be mistaken" as he held his bleeding hand to his side out of the view of the employee. Later when I asked why he told them it wasn't him that helped out, he said, "We don't seek gratitude for doing what we should do." I have tried never to forget that lesson.

My oldest son, when he was about 25 years old and was attending an annual employee recognition day at the warehouse where he works. He was part of a five man team doing a lot of heavy lifting all day long. All of his team except for him were married with children and working 12 – 16 hour days to earn a living for their families. To his surprise, my son was called forward to receive an award of $500.00, presented in five one hundred dollar bills, as well as a shiny new child's bicycle. He walked up to the front of the room where the "big boss" was standing and humbly accepted the rewards. Now my son didn't have a family to support but make no mistake, he was living payday to payday and barely making his mortgage payments. He walked back to where his team was standing and without saying a word, handed each of them a one hundred dollar bill, and then presented the bike to one of his mates that he knew had a child perfectly suited for the gift. The impact of his action no doubt sent a message of selflessness to all who observed and surely endeared him to his teammates as a leader.

This is one of my favorites because it is in my opinion the limitless trait that exemplifies the most honorable acts. Selflessness speaks to the very heart of who we are and it is portrayed by how we act and what we do for others without regard for personal reward or recognition. Selflessness can be achieved in a single act or it can be a lifetime pursuit, a calling if you will in service to others. Our Boy Scouts make service a central point of troop and individual achievement where service is defined as acts which support their community, school or church and each rank advancement includes a require-ment for service hours. Our boys also learn this in sports such as basketball where they are taught to pass the ball, let someone with a better opportunity score and be satisfied with an assist. In sports we can also see the polar oppo-site of selflessness when a football player makes a touchdown and goes about performing a dance routine that is obviously rehearsed bringing praise unto themselves for their supreme brilliance in action. I have to believe that if my sainted mother would ever see me conduct myself in such a manner she'd grab me by the ear and dress me down like no one's business.

After retiring from the Marine Corps we relocated to Rockwall Texas where by luck or destiny we happened to move next door to another military retiree by the name of Joseph P. Lynch and his lovely wife Connie. Joe and

Connie raised four young boys, now very successful men with families of their own. Joe and I not only shared the common bond of military service, we were also trained as artillerymen (commonly referred to as "Redlegs") at Ft. Sill OK and both of us had served in combat. As a young soldier Joe was serving in Vietnam as a crew chief and door gunner on a Huey helicopter Gunship assigned to a squadron given the prestigious call sign "Blue Max." During 16 – 17 April 1968 the 1st Battalion, 9th Marines at Khe Sanh while conducting search and destroy patrols were in one heck of a fight with a numerically superior North Vietnamese Army (NVA) unit during Operation Scotland II. After the fighting died down there were 19 Marines killed in action (KIAs) there were 46 serious wounded in action (WIAs) and 16 missing in action (MIAs) and unrecovered before the unit was able to break contact. The next day a Marine aerial observer reported sighting one Marine casualty at the scene of the battle who was still alive but he was now in the middle of enemy held territory. For hours medevac choppers tried repeatedly and unsuccessfully to land and rescue the Marine only to be fired at by a hailstorm of enemy small arms and rockets. Finally Blue Max, turning circles above the wounded Marines looking for a break in the firing so they could attempt a landing and in a hail of enemy fire was able to land one chopper, it was Joe Lynch's bird. Joe had just turned 19 years old and he had a bead on the Marine's location in the distance. Without regard for his personal safety Joe jumped out of the bird, sprinted to the downed Marine while under intense enemy fire and carried him back to the Huey where they were able to fly him to the Aid Station at Khe Sanh. For his actions on that day Joe would be awarded the Silver Star.

For years afterward Joe has tried to no avail to track down the identity of that Marine who he now believes was a young Corporal. Joe now volunteers his time mentoring veterans who have gone astray and landed on the wrong side of the law by working with them in the North Texas Regional Veteran's Court, the first of its kind in the nation. This court, manned by veteran mentors and presided over by Judge John Roach, himself a combat veteran of Desert Storm, is designed to give combat vets a second chance through a grueling program of rehabilitation which lasts approximately two years; a lifetime of selflessness.

In 2003 before we crossed the line of departure in the attack into Iraq, General Mattis addressed each of the 22,000 Marines and Sailors of the 1st Marine Division (it took him a few weeks but he addressed us all, unit by unit and in person). One of the messages he left us with was, "When you kill the enemy, and you will kill the enemy, act like you've done it before." His message was quite simple, the taking of a life is not an insignificant thing, we do so as a matter of necessity in the defense of our country and our ideals and it is not a moment for celebration. Be precise, methodical and efficient and "keep your honor clean" he would say. During the 16 plus years that our nation has been at war we have seen many young soldiers, sailors, airmen and Marines do some very heroic deeds to include some who have been awarded for their valor with our nation's highest award for valor, the Medal of Honor. In my 28 years of active duty and my ten years since retiring from active duty and working with several veterans organizations, I never heard a recipient of an award for valor brag about his or her exploits, on the contrary they are very humble and reluctant to talk about it. They were not seeking recognition during their heroic actions rather in most cases they acted in the best interest of the warrior to their left and right and the mission they were given. Now don't get me wrong, it's pretty entertaining to watch some of these touchdown dances but I have infinitely more respect for the player that scores a touchdown and points to the sky in deference to the Almighty, or simply hands the ball to the referee as if saying, no big deal, I've been in the end zone before and I'll be back again.

Selflessness can be taught, but it must be practiced to truly become a personal trait and then there are those few who act in a selfless manner instinctively and almost instantaneously such as the two young Marines then Lieutenant General John Kelly spoke of in a speech to the Semper Fi Society of St Louis on 13 November 2010 just four days after losing his own son in combat operations in Afghanistan. The General recounted the actions of two young Marines on duty guarding the vehicle access point to their outpost in Ramadi when an explosive laden vehicle attempted to enter the outpost with the intent of killing as many Marines and Iraqi police and soldiers as possible. The two Marines, 20 and 22 years old were from very different walks of life come together under the common bond of brotherhood as Marines. Explosive experts later estimated there was some 2000 pounds of explosives in the truck.

The only eye witnesses were Iraqi and they would say "Sir, in the name of God no sane man would have stood there and done what they did." "No sane man." Because when they saw the truck and immediately realized the deadly intent they all ran for their lives, all except these two Marines who had orders to guard this post and allow no unauthorized vehicles access. Video recovered from the blast showed that these Marines never stepped back, never even stepped aside, they planted their boots firmly, shouldered their weapons and unhesitatingly fired at the approaching vehicle until it stopped and detonated six seconds later. The selfless acts of these two young Marines saved the lives of over 160 Iraqi's. They would be nominated for our nation's second highest award for valor, the Navy Cross. As of the 27th of Jan 2017, the You Tube of General Kelly's speech had just over 20,000 "hits" while "Gangnam Style" had over 2.7 billion and Justin Beiber's "Sorry" had almost 2.2 billion. We have much to teach our boys.

As I said, this topic could have been an entire book and deservedly so. The single act of these two young Americans in a mere six seconds encapsulated so many fine traits such as honor, sacrifice, patriotism, courage, commitment, fortitude, strength, and words that simply do not begin to address the extraordinary character displayed by these Marines. This fortitude resides within the heart and soul of our boys, hopefully they will never have to display such extraordinary heroism to personify it, but if they can understand it to some degree, we are a better nation for it.

Selflessness begins with a state of mind, by serving others, by placing the needs of others before our own. Take your boys and volunteer for a park clean-up, a food drive or maybe just a visit to the nursing home where the elderly are always eager for a visitor. At the end of each day, ask your boy what he's done for someone other than himself. Each year on Memorial Day our Scout Troop gets up at 2:30 AM, dons their backpack and heads out to show their support for fallen veterans and first responders by marching in "Carry the Load." The boys march six miles with a backpack and a cardboard sign attached to it depicting the name of the veteran or first responder they are "carrying," a Grandfather, Uncle, Cousin or sometimes the name of someone they never knew. The premise is they carried us to the tune of ultimate sacrifice, the least we can do is go out and show support for their great sacrifice. I swell with pride at this act of selflessness and even more so when they race to carry the flags at the head of the column and refuse to give it up throughout the hike. These types of events cost nothing and the return on investment (time) is intangible.

Instill a sense of selflessness in your boys, incorporate a service day in your monthly routine where you spend maybe an hour or two helping someone or supporting a cause which brings them no monetary return or recognition. One of the great things about Boy Scouts is that in order for the boys to advance to each successive rank, they must perform hours of service to their church, community or school. The culminating requirement to achieve Eagle Scout is the Eagle Scout Project which also tasks the boy with planning and leading (not participating) a service project which will benefit their church, community or school. Some of my Scouts have led coat drives, built fences for community pools, benches for their schools and my youngest son Cannon's Eagle Scout project was to build a game table for a children's shelter. He also collected over twenty board games to donate as well. The idea came from our local Chief of Police who himself along with his wife donate much time and effort to helping support this very shelter. When Cannon went down to visit the shelter he immediately knew this was the project for him. There is plenty of opportunity to serve others, and it doesn't take much time or effort. People are most happy when they are doing something for others, help your boys be happy.

CHAPTER 9

ON FEAR

That single word which "real men" claim never to suffer. We recall such adages as President Franklin D. Roosevelt saying "Only thing we have to fear is fear itself." In his inaugural address, or "No Fear" on bumper stickers and T-shirts, or "Have no fear, Superman is here." Well, I am here to tell you fear is very real and just around every corner, it is how we deal with fear that sets one man apart from another. Fear is our natural alarm that warns us that something may be harmful to us. Fear is healthy and more importantly, fear is energy and energy is constant, never ending, always transferring until it reaches its potential, then it transfers. So, when we think about fear, we should think of it in the context of energy and how we can transfer that "energy" into a positive purpose. Marines are taught that fear on the battlefield must be transferred into action, for inaction will almost certainly lead to death.

Fear is a natural, instinctive and evolutionary function of the brain, more specifically of the amygdala region of the frontal cortex of the brain. The amygdala is the origin of emotions such as aggression, panic, anxiety and of course fear. This neurological mechanism has conditioned us to respond instinctively to danger such as the wild imagination of what could be lurking in the dark, or in my case, what swims around beneath me in the vast darkness of the open ocean. This natural form of self-preservation goes into hyper drive when faced with danger unless we train it to do otherwise.

As a young teen we went to go see the movie "Jaws" at the theater and I can't tell you if that was the moment I began to have a very real and visceral fear of the open water and more specifically, the ocean and sharks, but let's go ahead and assume that this was what did it for me. In the summer of 2015 I agreed to take a group of Scouts on a "High Adventure" trip to the Caribbean for a week of sailing which would take place in the summer of 2016. Well this was a full year away and my youngest son insisted he wanted to do this so, I raised my hand and said "I'll go as an adult leader." My wife maintains that is how I ended up in war zones so often, always too quick to raise my hand. Carefully calculating all the risks, I figured I'd be okay with snorkeling close to the shore so off we went to sail the great Atlantic.

On day two of our voyage on a 40 ft. sloop the six Scouts ages 14 - 17 and the other adult leader and I jumped off the boat we were living aboard and into the turquoise blue and crystal clear water for our morning of snorkeling. I drifted off to enjoy a particularly beautiful piece of coral when I realized I had drifted a bit far from the rest of the crew. I decided to head back towards them when the moment I turned I was face to face with a real live shark about five feet away from me and swimming directly towards me. My greatest fear had become a chilling reality, the mighty beast swam right beneath me and as I made a valiant and utterly unsuccessful attempt to walk on water, the great shark paid me not the least bit of attention and swam on (quite likely laughing at the pathetic display I put on). I got back to the boys running into my son Cannon first and I asked if he had seen the shark that just swam by them. He replied no and the other boys echoed, with a hint of doubt in their voice. By the time we got back to Texas, my shark tale grew, and so did the length of my shark. The mighty beast was at least 30 ft long, wearing a necklace, a monocle and top hat, and when he opened his mouth he had a "grill" that said "eat at Joe's."

This would not be my only encounter with fear on this trip. On the morning of day 4 the skipper informed us that we would be doing a "deep water coral combat dive" where we would all line up on the ship's rail in our snorkeling gear and as the boat was at full sail we would one by one drop into the water in a finely tuned military-like covert operation. The boys were excited and I could only remember the skipper saying "deep water." I already envisioned sharks wearing dinner napkins waiting in the "deep water." Just before the dive the skipper asked if anyone had a video camera because catching this event on video would be truly amazing for the boys to see. Being the quick thinking opportunist that I was, I quickly saw this as my way out of the "deep water" dive. I informed the skipper that I had a video camera and would be happy to archive this special event. The skipper said "Great Quint, what we're gonna do is make a first pass and drop you in the water, then make a big loop and swing back around to drop the boys in." Me and my big mouth, now I could see the great sharks scraping their knives and forks together and licking their lips. But I couldn't back out, the boys would never look at me the same again, I had to do it, I had to get my fear under control.

As I was putting on my gear, the fear in my gut was palpable. One of the Scouts who I have known for years and had a reputation as a "funny guy" was sitting next to me and in his best attempt at feigned moral support said, "Mr. Avenetti, don't worry, you'll be fine, those sharks are probably down there waiting for you, you know its feeding time right?" I pretended to ignore him but it didn't last long as he continued calmly, "Probably Tiger Sharks, they like to feed in the morning hours you know." I replied, "Lane, you have no idea." I made my way to the rail and stood ready to jump. The skipper hollered "Anytime you are ready Quint!" I couldn't wait or think I just had to jump! So, in I went, concentrating the whole time on getting my camera oriented and saying to myself, "Don't look down Avenetti, don't look down, just focus on the boat, focus on the boat," I was transferring my fear into action.

After what seemed like an hour but was likely only about 2 – 3 minutes the boat made its turn and was inserting the boys about 20 meter away from me. My anxiety level reduced and I had conquered my fear by focusing on capturing this special event on video for the boys and their parents. Would I do this again? Absolutely not, but that check mark is already on my bucket list along with "swim with sharks." Actually neither were on my bucket list but I did add them to bolster the thrill/danger level and of course to get credit.

During my Scoutmaster's Minute I used the story of my old Marine buddy Gunnery Sergeant Charles Restifo who I served with on Embassy duty in El Salvador in 1981 - 82. During Operation Desert Storm while serving with 1st Combat Engineer Battalion then Staff Sergeant Restifo would earn the Silver Star by leading his men crawling through an anti-personnel minefield on his hands and knees and probing the ground for mines with bayonets. His fear was turned into positive energy through taking action to ensure the safe passage of Marines through the extensive belts of anti-armor and anti-personnel minefields.

The difference between the fear I describe in my shark story and the fear of warriors in combat is actually quite different. The fear of warriors in battle does not emanate from fear of death or injury as most would believe and as historically has been documented until recently. LtCol. Dave Grossman's study of combat titled "On Killing" had a specific focus on the act of killing by soldiers and his study quite extensively covered all aspects of the psyche in relation to the act of killing and how warriors dealt with it after the act. I won't go into detail beyond his analysis of fear as a factor in combat. Interestingly, the biggest fear noted by warriors fresh out of combat was in letting their comrades down. You see, fear has many motivators and some of these motivators enable us, or drive us to extraordinary feats such as the heroic deeds of Gunnery Sergeant Restifo and Gunnery Sergeant Howard.

Fear is real, fear manifests in many forms such as; fear of illness, fear of death, fear of danger, or even fear of public speaking. Strangely, public speaking is said to be a greater fear, even than death. I recall my days at Marine Corps Recruiters School in San Diego in 1985 where we had a few combat veterans of the Vietnam War in our class. I watched these men who had braved the dangers of combat stand in front of their peers in a classroom to deliver a five minute impromptu speech physically shaking at the knees, voice quavering. These men were not cowards, far from it, they were proven combat veterans who had faced life and death situations but the prospect of public speaking truly terrified them.

Encourage your boys to face their fears, even if subtle fears, they must face them with energy and confidence and even if they fail, they will find the attempt liberating and strengthening. Challenge them to overcome just one fear at a time and you will see them grow before your eyes and more importantly, they will know that fear can be re-directed into positive energy such as the motivating fear of warriors letting each other down in combat, and they need fear not. The Marine Officer's Guide calls out "Ability to teach and speak usually denotes an effective leader and enhances whatever latent leadership talents you possess." Remind them that we control our mind, we control our actions and with the power of focus on the positive we can turn fear into positive action, in effect conquering fear, if only temporarily and this will inspire others. Very often, temporary conquest of fear is more than sufficient to win the day.

CHAPTER 10

ON INITIATIVE

As a young Marine I recall on several occasions my leaders saying "Lance Corporal Avenetti, good initiative, poor judgement." I had a knack for being quick to act without completely thinking through the 2nd and 3rd order effects of my actions. Initiative should always be coupled with judgement and accountability, we all want to be the first or best but we must instill in our boys the mindset of "what if." Thinking through the "what ifs" should not hinder initiative rather it should discipline initiative into actions that are well thought out and productive and of course they are then more apt to be accountable for their actions. Of course there are occasions where quick action is a must, such as someone choking, rescuing someone from an accident or when in combat. In the case of combat we rely on training, where actions are largely driven by repetitious training and muscle memory which serve to support initiative. First Responders train for the reaction to emergencies where they recognize conditions of an accident and respond accordingly and swiftly. We should not confuse training with initiative as training breeds muscle memory while initiative is a conscious and deliberate act, it is a choice.

During Operation Desert Shield a young Marine Reconnaissance Team Leader by the name of Charles Ingraham was holed up with his reconnaissance team in the Saudi border town of Kahfji when an Iraqi Mechanized Brigade crossed the border and seized the town. All Marine units were ordered to leave the town before the attack but Corporal Ingraham chose to stay and "do his job" reporting enemy activity. After a flurry of action where Pan-Arab forces attacked, then retreated, a column of enemy tanks entered the town right under the observation of Ingraham. Ingraham immediately called for a fire mission relayed through an OV-10 Bronco Marine aerial observation plane. The Bronco pilot relayed the call for fire to my artillery battalion sitting just south along the road to Kahfji. Making a long story short, we were able to respond to the call for fire from Ingraham and destroy the column of 14 tanks. Additionally, moments later, the survivors re-grouped and honed in on the Marine's position. Ingraham immediately called for a "repeat" of the mission which dispensed of the survivors. Of note, the grid coordinate for the mission was almost smack dab on top of his team's location, the young Marine had essentially signed his team's death warrant. Ingraham's initiative and bravery would earn him the Silver Star and no doubt the gratitude of his teammates for living to tell the story.

During the hours leading up to the U.S. and coalition forces attack into Iraq in 2003 the 1st Marine Division had made final plans for what was named "Opening Gambit" a series of coordinated artillery and air fires on key enemy units to clear the way for the division's Regimental Combat Teams (RCTs). Understand this was a very carefully scripted plan with timelines mapped out and all actions linked to another. A credible enemy report indicated that Iraqi forces were prepared to destroy the Gas Oil Separation Plants (GOSPs) and deny us the ability to secure their critical oil production capabilities which would be key in rebuilding a post war Iraq. Later our Pioneer Unmanned Air Vehicles (UAVs) confirmed Iraqi forces were setting fire to oil wells near the GOSP, the situation was now critical.

General Mattis who was in constant communication with higher headquarters and his subordinate commanders contacted the Commander of RCT 5 Colonel Joe Dunford (now Chairman of the Joint Chiefs of Staff) to advise him of the escalated timeline. Colonel Dunford was highly respected and almost revered by his Marines so much so that it was not uncommon for RCT 5 Hummers to be spotted with MRE box cardboard hanging from their front bumpers saying "Grizzly 6 for President." Grizzly being the call sign for 5th Marines and "6" indicating the Commander of 5th Marines. Not soon after advising Colonel Dunford of the expected timeline for moving into the attack, General Mattis called Dunford back and said, "Grizzly 6 this is Chaos (Chaos being General Mattis' call sign) how soon can you be ready to go?" "General, we can go now" came the reply. The order was issued, RCT 5 was to attack in zone to secure the critical oil infrastructure and isolate the Iraqi 51st Mechanized Division. "Chaos" instinctively understood the critical importance of seizing the initiative and acted accordingly. Dunford also knew the importance of being ready to capitalize on opportunity or respond to his commander's initiative. This initiative likely saved the valuable resources the Iraqi nation would need to rebuild.

Give your boys a task but don't tell them how to do it rather, share with them your vision. Vision communicates what you expect as the completed task and allows your boys to think independently and take initiative. Allow them to formulate a plan upon their own initiative. The plan may be flawed and the outcome may not be ideal but the exercise in initiative will be invaluable. Critique his action afterward and offer counsel in critical thinking and in the decision making process, there will be plenty of teaching points which offer opportunity to point out the "what ifs." Initiative with poor judgment should not be admonished, it should be critiqued, discussed and used as a lesson from which to build. Eventually your boy will develop ever increasing initiative along with better judgment. Remember, even if you end up telling them "good initiative, poor judgment," much like Lance Corporal Avenetti, there is yet hope for them.

CHAPTER 11

ON ACCOUNTABILITY

"It wasn't my fault." We hear these words roll off the tongues of our teens with such ease that it is almost as if they practice it, and perhaps they do. It takes a conscious effort to reinforce the behavior of personal accountability because we see and hear it from national figures so often on television or in tweets and other forms of social media. It has almost become okay to explain away our errors or mistakes by simply saying "It wasn't my fault." We see Presidential candidates and former high level executives shirk responsibility and blame as quickly as an old west gunfighter pulls out his six gun, "It's not my fault." The sad part is that they have probably clawed their way to the top by doing exactly that their whole lives and getting away with it. In order for our boys to grow into young men of honor they must learn accountability, slow to accept credit, quick to accept responsibility, even when it may not be entirely their fault.

My second son Gunner, an Eagle Scout decided to join the Air Force last year after graduating high school, we don't need to discuss the sentiments of a Marine Dad when his son decides not to join the Marine Corps; but seriously it was a very proud moment to watch my son choose to serve his country and I was supremely honored to swear him in with the oath of enlistment. Anyway, he calls on a regular basis and one evening tells us he has been assigned as Dormitory "Floor Chief" and that he has to take accountability. I asked him what this entailed and he replied that he had to receive the report from each Hall Chief and compile them into a comprehensive report.

I reminded him that taking accountability meant that he was accountable for the actions or inactions of the personnel on his floor. What they do and what they fail to do under his charge such as failing to clean their rooms or common areas would be his responsibility, he is accountable for their success and more importantly their failures, not simply their presence, such is the weight of leadership.

In the 1990's there was an incident at the Marine Corps Air Ground Combat Center (MCAGCC) at Twenty-nine Palms, CA. A young Marine was placed on a road guard detail during a live fire exercise to ensure no one inadvertently wandered into the impact area. Through a litany of errors and irresponsible actions by the officer responsible for the road guards, the young Marine was placed in the wrong spot and never recovered after the end of the exercise and his absence was not reported for over 40 hours after the exercise ended. The responsible officer failed in his accountability for personnel under his charge and in this case failure in accountability came with dire consequences, the death of a young Marine. Accountability does not end with the person placed in charge, it goes up the chain to all with vested responsibility and the Marine Corps swiftly discharged punitive action all the way to the young Marines battalion commander. Accountability and responsibility go hand in hand.

I work to instill in my Scouts as well as my sons the weight and importance of accountability because I have seen too closely the ramifications of lackadaisical leadership. Such casual tasks as taking role call before and after activities or campouts instill a sense of accountability in young boys and a story such as this serve to remind them of the importance of their position of responsibility. It should be noted that our Boy Scout Troop uses the "Boy Led" method of Scouting which places the boys in all positions of responsibility within the troop. The adult leaders are there to observe, counsel and guide the boys in their actions to ensure safety and mentor them but not to intervene, even, and especially if it means watching the boys fail.

Hold your boys accountable for their actions as well as their inactions. Teach them about the consequences of their actions and that personal responsibility must always be considered first before looking elsewhere for blame. Mentor them in the weight of leadership; if the team fails, then the leader has failed them. In failure, a leader must first examine and accept blame for his shortcomings and then take corrective action. There is nothing worse than a leader or team captain chewing out his team for a loss while refusing to accept personal accountability. Teach them that actions must be considered before taken, problems must be framed before solved in a manner which presents the facts and creates an enhanced understanding of the challenge at hand. Using this framing as the entry arguments, they should formulate courses of action and evaluate each course in their mind before implementing them. You may think this an arduous task for something as simple as making a decision but in reality, we do this almost every time we make decisions, we have just learned to do it in a compressed timeline. This process gives confidence that we have given due diligence to our decisions and encourages us to take accountability for our actions. If they are in a position of leadership they should also remember to share accountability for success with their team, never missing an opportunity to praise them in public while counseling individual failures in private and in a teacher – scholar fashion. Nothing sours a team faster than a leader who places blame on everyone but himself.

CHAPTER 12

ON FAILURE

I t seems that the word failure has taken on a completely negative conno-
tation in our modern lexicon while quite the opposite should be considered during the formative years of our youths. We tell our kids that they
cannot fail their classes, cannot fail in sports, and we fear failure so much so
that we now hand out participation certificates rather than point out that one
participant actually wins and the others who do not win or failed to win, in
other words they lost. Some schools no longer issue the "F" grade for failing a
class for fear that we will stigmatize the young student and damage their sense
of self-worth. To lose or to fail is not final, it is not the end of the world and
we should recognize that through failure we often learn our most important
lessons. When your kids learned to ride a bike, at some point you had to let
go and watch him pedal away happily or fall over, skin his knee, maybe cry
a bit, but get right back on armed with the lesson of pain if he doesn't maintain balance. Now with a new resolve and firm mindset to succeed, he will
eventually be riding like a champ. Failure propels us to strive, to improve, to
achieve and ultimately to win.

As a Targeting Officer for the 1st Marine Division in the invasion of
Iraq in 2003 I had ample opportunity to succeed and even more opportunity
to fail. My failures were not for lack of trying nor lack of due diligence to my
trade but sometimes things just don't quite align, the enemy gets a vote and
a target has a lucky day and survives to fight again. My recollection of the
many memories of combat somehow seem to center on the targeting missions

where I failed to adequately address my target because I would turn the event over and over in my mind trying to figure out what went wrong or what I could have done better. My professional curiosity and obligation to excellence as a Marine compelled me to dissect my failures and improve processes where possible or propose changes to technology where applicable. I continued this pursuit of improved technology and techniques in my subsequent career in the defense industry. Honestly, my successes did not drive me to such professional pursuit rather, it has been my failures which have driven me.

We've all heard of Thomas Edison and his invention of the light bulb. Well, most accounts posit that Edison failed 10,000 times before he got it right. Well that might not be entirely accurate but according to an interview Edison gave Harper's Monthly Magazine in 1890 he claimed to have "constructed 3000 different theories with connection on electronic light." Yet in only two cases did his theory prove true. The adage here is apparent, we learn from our failures and we must allow our boys to learn from theirs. Let them scrape their knees, let them try their hand at something new, just watch and guide, counsel and suggest but let their creative and inquiring mind wander and explore, you just might see the light bulb go on (pun intended).

While backpacking across the Rockies with a crew of six Scouts, each day a different Scout was in charge of navigating, or as we fondly called it "*navi-guessing*." The boys were armed with a map and a compass, no GPS or other navigational aids beyond what we taught them such as how to read a map, terrain association and pace counting. Not only were we teaching them the important skill of land navigation but more importantly we wanted them to build self-confidence and learn to deal with failure. Taking a wrong turn on a trail was a very real possibility, especially when there were more than one trail option close to each other. We let them get just a bit down the wrong path before hinting that they may want to re-check their map. If they weren't allowed to fail, they would not know how to deal with failure nor would they have a chance to learn from their mistakes. This ten day backpacking trek is one of the most memorable experiences of my life and to spend it with my youngest son was even more rewarding.

Allow your boys to make mistakes, let them fail, let them fall down from time to time, especially in instances where the ramifications are not severe. We have all heard of helicopter moms, well I have seen helicopter dads as well. The last thing your boy wants or needs is you hovering over him to protect him from failure, or make excuses for him when he does fail. Remember, the lesson is in the failing, there is no teachable moment if we correct before failure or worse yet, excuse away the failure as someone else's fault. Watch them as they fail, careful not to admonish them rather, use the failure as teachable moment so that you can mentor them through "right." If they are afraid to fail, they will never take chances, they will never experience the limits of their capability nor will they ever advance to greater pursuits. Use your judgment and experience to anticipate where you might need to interdict for risk of injury to self or others. Explain the potential for severe consequences should they have continued on the wrong trail, and how they could have considered other course of action to reach the desired end state. The last thing you want is to make them afraid to attempt the difficult for fear of failure. Always leave them with encouraging words and a positive spirit.

CHAPTER 13

ON PATRIOTISM

Patriotism, we like to fly that word just like a flag, we drop it whenever we get a chance and all of us, with small exception grab hold of it as if we have sole proprietorship of all it represents. We love to claim to be patriots and say we have patriotism and yet when it comes right down to it, we all have slightly different definitions of patriotism. Some would simply say love of country, while others may say belief in our nation, or support for our military and veterans. Merriam Webster defines it as: "love that a person feels for his or her country." The problem with this very subjective definition is that it infers the word "feels." Who is to say that what I feel is any more patriotic than what you feel? So let's talk briefly on patriotism.

I watch in disgust as national sports figures sit while the National Anthem is played and they claim to do this in the name of patriotism, they feel their actions are right and just and proclaim to love this country yet it conflicts directly with my upbringing and beliefs as well as the beliefs of most Americans. If we accept the subjective nature of patriotism then we have to allow these heinous displays of disrespect to go on, and by law we must allow them to go on. What occurs to me is that these individuals who just happen to have the national stage by virtue of their fame (deserved or otherwise) have never laid their life on the line for the ideals this great nation represents nor the freedoms they so brazenly and presumptuously enjoy. Let's take for instance the love a mother has for her baby; they protect and nurture that baby especially when they are sick, they don't sleep, they stress and worry and no one but that mother can realize just how deep that love is because they have not carried that baby in their womb or labored through child birth for the infant. If someone were to try and harm that baby that mother would go to the ends of the earth to ensure no harm befalls their child, such is the love of a mother for her child and such is the love of country many of us who have fought for it feel.

There was a piece of C-Ration cardboard found in the besieged firebase of Khe San during the Vietnam War and on it an unknown author had inscribed; "Life has a special flavor for those who fight for it that the protected never know." This special flavor can also be applied to patriotism, where for those who have fought for it, the love of country is special, and watching such displays of disrespect are hurtful at a very deep level and I might add that many who have not fought for it have an equally passionate love for country. We know this act will not diminish the strength of our great nation in any way however, the disregard for the "feelings" of others served no useful purpose beyond self-gratification. A true patriot will find other ways of protesting. We must build in our young boys a sense of ownership in this country, we all have a vested interest in our continued success and our collective pride serves as a shield to any threats. The intangible strength of patriotism while untouchable, nevertheless sends a loud and clear message that we will fight tooth and nail to protect this great nation.

We have all heard of Patrick Henry, that famous name but wait, why was he famous? Don't worry, many Americans know the name however, few can tell you what brought fame to this early American patriot. Faced with increasing British military presence in the American colonies, Henry beseeched the continental congress on March 23, 1775 to fight for the liberties they so desired, he supplicated himself to the degree that he offered his life in this supremely important fight for freedom, "Give me liberty or give me death." Imagine, if you will, anything that you would lay your life down for, your children no doubt, but a purpose? Not likely. When we take into account that less than 1% of the American populace serves in the military and the majority of Americans have little to no knowledge of the military or how it functions, we now gain perspective. Patrick Henry was willing to lay down his life for this intangible purpose of liberty for himself and his soon-to-be nation.

Patriotism need not be as grand as Patrick Henry, it can be found in the actions of every good citizen in their own way. When a Boy Scout aspires to the esteemed rank of Eagle Scout, he must, as a culmination to his ascent plan, execute and complete a service project which benefits either the community, a school or a religious institution. Many of the Eagle Scout candidates I have coached/mentored over the years have chosen patriotic projects such as young Josh Hargrove refurbishing the flags which the American Legion displays around the historic Rockwall County courthouse, or Andrew Hildebrand planning and supporting the 75th anniversary tribute to veterans of Pearl Harbor, or identifying, mapping and recognizing grave sites of veterans with American flags on Memorial Day and Veterans Day completed by young Ben Haury.

What can you do now? Teach your boys to stand proud when the flag passes by in a parade, or when the National Anthem is played and to put their hand over their heart in a show of respect. There is no better opportunity to do this than at a school athletic event. Patriotism does not have to be overt, it can be humble, silent and proud with no need to thump their chest. Some prefer the loud method and I am okay with that, they fly the flag in the back of their pick-up trucks, wave it on a stick during parades or place flag stickers all over their vehicles. All this is good but action always speaks louder than words, show them how to act. Volunteer alongside your son in a community service project, there are plenty to choose from and many of them take place during holidays or weekends to accommodate work hours. Attend your local Veterans Day or Memorial Day tributes and you will undoubtedly walk away with a renewed sense of patriotism. Patriotism begins at home and extends from there.

CHAPTER 14

ON CITIZENSHIP

What has citizenship got to do with character and leadership you might ask? Of the thirteen merit badges a Boy Scout is required to earn for advancement to Eagle Scout, three deal with citizenship; Citizenship in the Community, Citizenship in the Nation and Citizenship in the World. Surely this emphasis on citizenship must have some importance in character development. Merriam Webster defines citizenship as "the status of being a citizen, or the quality of an individual's response to membership in a community." It is this latter definition that we will focus on for it brings with it the association of "quality" which goes beyond the mere entitlement of being a citizen. With citizenship comes responsibility, responsibility to abide by laws, to be a good neighbor, and a contributing payer of taxes for the greater good of the community. It is these obligations which we must instill in our boys, a sense of commitment to the greater needs and good order of the masses for without it, we are merely a mob void of order or process.

We claim to be citizens of our community, citizens of our state and citizens of our nation while there are also those who claim to be citizens of the global community. We can view citizenship as the individual contributions to the greater society in which they live and partake, and if we view this as a societal issue, should we not also visit what and how we can contribute to the needs of our democratic society? After all, if we take from the society, should we not also give back to the society? And if we think of this as a give and take relationship or a shared responsibility not just for the sustainment but for the improvement of our democracy then we must recognize the importance of citizenship as a shared calling at all societal levels. There should be no doubt, citizenship in this great nation is indeed a privilege and should never be taken for granted, nor bestowed upon anyone seeking it through illegal or nefarious means.

Former Secretary of State Condoleeza Rice in her recent book "*Democracy, Stories from the Long Road to Freedom*" compiles a study of how democracies emerge or "come" and the intense work required to sustain and grow her. While we privileged Americans enjoy the fruits of our fore father's labor and sacrifice we must observe the stark contrast between a life in democracy as compared to a life in say a totalitarian regime such as the former Soviet Union or Benito Mussolini's Italy. The totalitarian regime promises that the government will provide for the masses where democracy requires that the population partake in the structure and vibrancy of the nation. This then is the essence of citizenship, where we citizens are vested with this wonderful gift of America yet we must work to maintain and sustain her.

The hallmark of citizenship is in community service. Community service comes in many colors and flavors such as Volunteer Firefighters, community clean-up events, service based organization that contribute to the greater good through not for profit activities such as Boy Scouts of America and church youth groups. There are many veteran organizations that give back through youth leadership development such as the American Legion who sponsors Boys State and Girls State, teaching high school age youths how a democratic style state government functions as a subset to the greater constitutional republic. In effect, the best way to become a good or better citizen is through the study of our governmental processes and participating in some of the many methods of contributing to your community or nation.

Author Sebastian Junger in his recent book "*Tribe*" opines that "a fundamental lack of connectedness allows people to act out in trivial but incredibly selfish ways. Junger's work studies the tribal nature of ancient and some not so ancient societies in an effort to understand the cohesiveness and harmony of a society and how such harmony can be broken or interrupted perhaps irreparably. My experience as a Marine taught me the value of a the tribal community or society where closeness, inclusiveness and shared responsibilities create a team mentality where we police up each other and all work toward the betterment of the tribe. Junger's work makes stark comparison between military personnel (tribal living) separating from service and re-integrating into society where there is a distinct lack of tribal living. We could all be well served to view citizenship as a calling to unite as a community, state and nation for the mutual betterment and common good. We need look no further than our own Constitution which opens by calling for a "more perfect Union, establish justice, insure domestic Tranquility, provide for the common defence, promote the general Welfare and secure the blessings of liberty," similarly, these are the unwritten mandates of the tribe.

When I was a student in high school we had a class called "Civics" and if we study the definition of "civics" we find that Merriam Webster defines it simply as "the study of the rights and duties of citizens and of how government works." This seems pretty straight forward and simple, but in reality, if we were to ask a typical high school student what civics means, most would likely shrug their shoulders in doubt. Whether by divine providence or by chance, we were born to this great nation and we share an obligation to study and commit in our own way to making it better for following generations. Recall that a nation which does not study and know its history and mistakes are doomed to repeat them. Most recently we see demonstrations throughout the nation where some ill-conceived activists are attempting to tear down or do away with historical statues and monuments. This baseless act serves no tangible purpose beyond hiding our nation's history. Good or bad, our history is our history and it must be visible, accessible and undeniable in order for us to study and understand it. A nation that does not learn from its history will surely cease to be a nation. It is incumbent upon each of us as citizens to study our history, mistakes and all so that we can forge ahead smarter and stronger than our predecessors.

Some say that citizenship is a right that we are entitled to by virtue of birth, but we must also consider that many people throughout the world wait for years simply to have a chance at U.S. citizenship. We take for granted just how good we have it here in these United States, present company included, while one trip to a 3rd world country will bear witness to just how great it is to be an American Citizen. Citizenship should be seen as a privilege, a gift we so cherish that we would be willing to earn it each and every day. A gift so grand that many have laid down their lives for its preservation. While at my son Gunner's graduation from Air Force Basic Military Training at Lackland

Air Force Base in San Antonio, Texas the graduation ceremony included the oath of citizenship to eight graduates who were foreign nationals. This is important to note because the United States places such emphasis on service that during declared times of hostility, members of the U.S. Armed Forces who serve honorably (even 1 day) are eligible for naturalization under section 329 of the Immigration and Nationality Act, so long as they meet the defined requirements. Yet we watch the news as illegal immigrants protest at being unfairly treated. Citizenship is not a right, it is a privilege, a privilege paid for and insured in blood.

If we then say that U.S. citizenship must be legally earned, then we must be prepared to take a stance on those who enter our country illegally, enjoy the rights and privileges of citizenship while failing to adhere to the very laws we as citizens are expected to abide by. If we treat citizenship as a privilege, we are more apt to appreciate how lucky we are and how those foreign nationals who apply and wait (often for years) for legal citizenship truly deserve the title "United States Citizen." If your son steals a television, is it truly his television? If your son sneaks into the movie theater without buying a ticket, is he really entitled to be there? When we come by things of value without working for them, does not the perception of value diminish? For those that have not learned what it means to be an American Citizen we will find them more willing to abrogate the very value system this great nation was built upon, and it is happening now under our very noses. This will be the beginning of the erosion of who we are, just as the Romans saw their republic die a painful death, never again to rise. Yet, we have grown to ignore the millions who have illegally entered our country and enjoy the privileges we work to earn every day. They protest our governmental system as if they have rights of citizenship and protections under the very constitution we have sworn to defend. This, is not citizenship, it is thievery.

Our founding fathers gifted us this honor of citizenship through blood and lives lost in a world changing fight for freedom. This thing we call citizenship is not ours to give away without regard to rule of law. Teach your boys the value of true and honest citizenship and encourage them to stand up for it and earn it daily, it should never be taken for granted, nor frivolously given away. Visit historical monuments and sites, explore national parks and see what this great nation has to offer. Given the opportunity, visit the battlefield of Gettysburg or if not able, read a book about the Civil War such as

Killer Angels, this will give you and your son a new appreciation for the value of citizenship and the extent of commitment it takes to preserve this great nation. Read the constitution with your son, this very short document carries such foresight, such wisdom and such understanding of human nature that it will survive a millennia... unless we forget its purpose. Thomas Jefferson famously said; "We in government do not have government by the majority – we have government by the majority who participate... All tyranny needs to gain a foothold is for people of good conscience to remain silent. Take your son to your next city council meeting and let him see government by the people in action and if what you see is anything but this, recall Thomas Jefferson's words. In the most basic act of citizenship, teach them not to litter, nothing says "I don't belong" than someone throwing their trash on our shared sidewalks and finally remember the words of our 1st President George Washington, "The Constitution of the United States ...its only keepers, the people."

CHAPTER 15

ON HONOR

When we discuss honor, we must keep in mind a sacred obligation, an obligation or agreement which places one's integrity and personal value at stake. When we shake the hand of an important or influential person we might say, "It is an honor to meet you" because we want to convey the degree to which we value the occasion. Honor is a word which carries distinction and noteworthiness, a sense of uniqueness which is rarely equaled or surpassed. When I met then Vice President George H. W. Bush while serving at the U.S. Mission in Geneva Switzerland in 1983 I said, "It is an honor Sir" and I truly meant it. An honor should be something that is rarely bestowed upon someone such as to be ordained a Bishop, knighted as a Knight, or promoted the rank of General, those selected for these positions are few and typically stand out among their peers. I am reminded of a line in the movie "Gladiator" where actor Russell Crowe playing the Roman General Maximus turned slave and then Gladiator would come face to face in the coliseum with his nemesis Caesar. He would look him in the eye and say "The time for honoring yourself will soon be at an end… Highness." The message is clear, when we honor ourselves, we will never truly have honor. Honor is in the eye of the beholder and can only be bestowed, not assumed.

Boy Scouts take an oath when they say "On my honor" which signifies the ultimate allegiance and obligation to fulfil the charges taken in the oath. To acquit one's self with honor signifies performance above and beyond whether it is on the field of battle or service to one's community or cause and it is a good thing to be honored. Honor cannot be self-bestowed, in order for honor to have meaning it must be bestowed by the observer or those entrusted with keeping the integrity of the particular honor. And even after all this we can still agree that a young boy can have honor, live a life worthy of honor although teenage boys typically have other things on their mind. The Marine Corps specifies "Honor, Courage and Commitment" as their core values. How and why does honor become one of the three values deemed most important to our Corps of Marines? Let's explore this further.

When we crossed the line of departure in the attack into Iraq in March, 2003 with the 1st Marine Division, our Commanding General, General Mattis, a man of great honor would ensure all personnel in his division received a letter he himself drafted entitled "Commanding General's Message to All Hands." Within this letter he set the tone for what would be the most extensive and massive attack by American Forces since the Korean War. In this letter he would place honor at the center of his mandate by directing that we treat all who do not resist with "decency, demonstrating chivalry and sol-dierly compassion." He further directed that we should "use good judgement and act in the best interests of our Nation." Finally he would ask that we "Fight with a happy heart and strong spirit" and above all in honor of those who have fought under the colors of the 1st Marine Division to "keep your honor clean" words he purposely chose from the revered Marine's Hymn. You see, honor in the context of action, is purity of purpose and when we send young American men into battle we must provide them with purity of purpose because they are about to commit such violent and tenacious acts in the name of freedom, many of them will be scarred for life.

Medal of Honor recipient Desmond Doss recently portrayed in the motion picture *Hacksaw Ridge* is a shining example of a man maintaining honor against insurmountable odds. Doss, who knew he must answer the call to service for his country, stood on his faith, his value system and his moral compass throughout basic training and through combat operations where most anyone else would have abandoned their position out of convenience. Doss was surrounded by tormentors who threatened him, beat him and pres-sured him into abandoning his faith because it did not fall in line with their value system. During the battle for Okinawa, the last Japanese island battle before the allied forces would have to attack the mainland itself, the Japanese defended like mad men. Throughout the battle for Hacksaw Ridge Doss would repeatedly make trips while unarmed, braving withering enemy fire to retrieve wounded comrades. This unprecedented feat is almost unimaginable for an armed soldier, Doss was armed only with his faith and with his honor; talk about courage, integrity, character!

In essence, our boys can have no honor if we do not teach them what is honorable, such as honorable behavior or actions as well as what is not honorable or without honor. Honor is earned without expectation of same, for honor without humility is misplaced and destined to fall. We have heard the expression from Proverbs 16:18 "pride goeth before destruction, and haughty spirit before a fall." When we demand honor, or honor ourselves we lose the respect of all who observe us regardless of how honorable our actions may have been. If an honorable act is committed with no one to observe, is it any less honorable? Likewise, if an honorable action is taken and those who observe it do not make honorable mention, is the act any less honorable? Humility must be the counter-balance to honor, hand-in-hand they move forward until our actions are honorable without expectation of accolades, rewards or glory, they are simply honorable and you have achieved honor. Honor - vivid consciousness of personal dignity and worth. The Bushido code passed down from the ancient Japanese Samurai speaks of honor in the form of eight virtues which combined comprise the character traits of a man of honor. The code of Bushido taught that it was the man's obligation to teach his children moral standards through the model of his own behavior. Set the example of honor for your boys, act honorably and they will emulate this.

Author with Boy Scouts from Troop 989 at 2015 Rockwall County
Memorial Day event Front row L-R: Cade Edwards, Conner
Manning, Cannon Avenetti, Author, Jase Trahan; Back row L-R:
Bradley Mitchell, Gunner Avenetti, Logan Green, Brennan Manning,
Brendan Shew, Mason Woolbright (*Courtesy Quint Avenetti*)

Corporal Quint Avenetti and then Vice President George H.W.
Bush, U.S. Mission, Geneva, Switzerland 1983, 3rd from left
in front row next to V.P. (*Courtesy Quint Avenetti*)

Boy Scout Troop 989, 14 of 23 Scouts pictured are
now Eagle Scouts (*Courtesy Quint Avenetti*)

Author with First Lady Barbara Bush during Operation Desert Shield/Storm, Thanksgiving 1990 What a scolding she gave me! (*Courtesy Quint Avenetti*)

Josh Hargrove Eagle Scout Project Refurbishing American Flags for Historic Rockwall County Courthouse sponsored by American Legion, Terry Fisher Post 117 (*Courtesy Quint Avenetti*)

Author's sons: L-R Gunner, Cannon, Quint at Cannon's Eagle
Scout Court of Honor May 2016 (*Courtesy Quint Avenetti*)

Medal of Honor recipient Mike Thornton with author's sons Gunner and Cannon and friend Wilson (*Courtesy Quint Avenetti*)

Troop 989 ready to "Carry the Load" 6 mile hike at 3:00 AM, Memorial Day 2015 and continued each year since (*Courtesy Quint Avenetti*)

Scouts from Troop 989 white water rafting in the Colorado Rockies July 2015 (*Courtesy Quint Avenetti*)

Teens participating in American Legion, Terry Fisher Post 117 sponsored
Youth Leadership Symposium May 2017 *(Courtesy Quint Avenetti)*

Artillery Fires, Operation Iraqi Freedom March, 2003. Artillery
was devastating and accurate. (*Courtesy Quint Avenetti*)

Religious service during Iraqi Freedom, faith is critical in life, especially in combat. (*Courtesy Quint Avenetti*)

Eagle Scout Board of Review for Charlie Warren, he made it! (*Courtesy Quint Avenetti*)

Cannon Avenetti Eagle Scout Project (Game Table) benefiting Kaufman County TX Children's Advocacy Center (*Courtesy Quint Avenetti*)

The Author, older brother Nick (Eagle Scout) and Dad (Scoutmaster) 1976 (*Courtesy Quint Avenetti*)

Author with son Gunner new Eagle Scout Nov 2015. Ethos and values of U. S. Marines mirror closely with Boy Scouts. (*Courtesy Quint Avenetti*)

Author (digging) and Sgt Uloa, (*left*) "Digging In" Desert
Shield/Storm 1990 (*Courtesy Quint Avenetti*)

Gene Cernan (last man to walk on the moon), son Gunner,
U.S. Congressman Ralph Hall, Author - 2016 Rockwall
Band of Brothers (*Courtesy Quint Avenetti*)

Author with son Cannon backpacking in the Rockies with Boy Scouts at Philmont Scout Ranch July 2015 (*Courtesy Quint Avenetti*)

Scouts at Sea Base St Thomas U.S. Virgin Islands 6 days of live aboard sailing, July 2016! L-R Brennan Manning, Michael Norwood, Jaxon Selman, Cannon Avenetti, Lane Pollock, Jarred Manning, Not pictured; Author and Todd Manning (*Courtesy Quint Avenetti*)

Scouts touring Artillery Museum, Ft Sill OK March 2015 L-R: Amoruso Helms-Smart "Ammo," Cannon, Gunner. Note the background "The ammo, the Cannon & the Gunner" (*Courtesy Quint Avenetti*)

Cannon Avenetti Spar Pole climbing, Philmont Scout
Ranch July 2015, (*Courtesy Quint Avenetti*)

Gunner Avenetti learning to fold the American flag,
very important 2008 (*Courtesy Quint Avenetti*)

Summiting Mt Phillips, 11,700 Ft. Philmont Scout Ranch July
2015 L-R: Scott Stockburger, Dean Manasco, Baxter Stockburger,
Author, Cannon Avenetti, Mason Woolbright, Logan Green,
Jack Hittson-Smith, Kevin Smith (*Courtesy Quint Avenetti*)

Walking with Mom during her Cancer fight L-R Nick Avenetti, Samson
Avenetti, Author, Mom Christina Armenta (not pictured brother
Guy Avenetti, Sister Valerie Jordan (*Courtesy Quint Avenetti*)

Author with Mom after winning first bout "Cancer
free!" (*Courtesy Quint Avenetti*)

Troop 989 supporting "Wreaths across America" L-R back: Bradley Mitchell, Jack Hittson-Smith, Raphael Hoel, Alan Apolinar, Lance Johnson, Jarred Manning, Evan Apolinar. L-R front: Jase Trahan, Josh Selman, Kyle Blackburn, Cannon Avenetti, Ben Morton, Jaxon Carpenter

Author with neighbor Joe Lynch CW3 USA (Ret)
Silver Star recipient (*Courtesy Quint Avenetti*)

With The Great General, 1st Marine Division (Forward) Camp Commando, Kuwait, Christmas 2002. L-R CWO5 Kevin DeLuca, CWO4 Quint Avenetti, Major General James N. Mattis, Capt. Samson Avenetti

Cannon Avenetti Eagle Scout Board of Review. L-R: Joe Lynch, Alan Smith, Kresha Alvarado, Cannon, Bobby Boedeker, John Edwards

CHAPTER 16

ON MIND, BODY & SPIRIT

The triad. These three essential components to living an honorable life ask that we pay attention to maintaining them all equally least one become weak and the tripod they jointly comprise to ensure a good life topple over from imbalance. I group them because they jointly combine to form the nucleus of who we are and what we stand for. This therefore is the balance of life, to be maintained equally and proactively rather than reactively. We'll examine each one separately and then come back to analyze them as a triad and what you can do to influence these fundamental aspects.

Mind. As legendary UCLA basketball coach John Wooden famously said; "It's what you learn after you know it all that counts." Isn't it great when your boys tells you "I know Dad." And you know full well that he doesn't but such is the mind of our young boys. We send our children to school in the hopes that they will study, learn and enhance their knowledge. We trust, and trust is a big word, that our schools will apply a curricula we approve of and our children will apply mental rigor in the development of this important leg of the tripod however, if we simply leave it to the schools to do this, we are missing a very important component to development of the mind. The mind encompasses substance well beyond simple reading, writing and arithmetic, it should include the formation of a value system which supports moral and ethical actions and decisions. Most do not realize this but the mission of the Boy Scouts of America is quite short and simple; "To prepare young people to make ethical and moral choices over their lifetime by instilling in them the values of the Scout Oath and Law." This is a simple mission but it says quite a bit about how important the moral and ethical mindset is and how a value system is intrinsic to a boy of strong character.

The knowledge base of our boys is developed largely in school however, this knowledge base does more than set the conditions for book learning, it is the precursor to the construct of the deeper mind and how we perceive life and the world around us. Ultimately, we expect and hope that our boys will extend their knowledge and life experiences into that elusive nirvana known as wisdom. We must take an interest in what our boys are being taught and the mentors being placed in front of them. What are the social settings they participate in and what kind of friends do they keep? Is the right answer to tell them who they can befriend, or what they can read? Not necessarily, we as parents must guide them along their path with the benefit of our life experience and wisdom. Whether your expectations for your boy are different than mine or anyone else's makes no difference, what is important is that you participate in this development. Suggest some quality books outside of school that may fall in line with their interests, or even a movie that may strike a chord with their imaginative side. Fiction, non-fiction, it makes no difference because reading stimulates the mind whether it be knowledge of medicine or the imagination of a fairy tale. This is a small step and wholly insufficient in and of itself, but it is a start, a start in taking an interest in their life. We'll talk more about this later in this section.

The mind also requires constant stimulation to continue to be nimble and perform at optimum levels however, most important to the health of our brain is rest. We can treat it like an automobile that needs servicing at regular intervals based on usage. Similarly, the mind needs constant stimulation through mental exercise and challenges and after all this, sleep is the oil change for the mind, something most teens are averse to. As I joined the Marine Corps at 17 years of age, obviously I never attended college or university. Now the Marine Corps offers all sorts of benefits to advance one's academic studies such as tuition assistance and of course the G.I. Bill. My personal choice was to apply my every energy into being the best Marine I could possibly be, going to every technical school I could go to, taking correspondence courses that interested me, but I never attempted to pursue a degree while in uniform. I did however, decide to pursue my bachelor's degree after retiring from the Corps, the problem with this was that I had to juggle a full time job, duties as Scoutmaster for a Troop that grew from 30 to 60 boys, as well as obligations as a husband and father and other veterans organizations which support youth development. Now don't shed a tear for me because I thoroughly enjoyed every bit of it, mental stimulation at school, activities of working with our youth and the fun of actually being home to get to know my family; win – win - win. We are never too old to learn.

Body. Now well into my fifties, I work out nearly every day, some days at 5:00 AM, other days in the evening but one way or another, I will get my workout in. The Marine Corps instilled in me the importance of good physical conditioning, and I have sought to continue this regimen of physical exertion in my post Marine Corps life. My boys have asked me why I work out so much, my response; "I have to earn the title of Marine every day." Being a United States Marine was a tremendous source of pride to me and when I was growing up I saw those lean, mean looking men in dress blues as if they were super men. As I transitioned from enlisted to officer I realized the importance of being physically fit especially if I expected to lead Marines, many of which were in extraordinarily tip top shape. The Marine Officer's Guide assesses the importance of "physical readiness, though not an end in itself, is essential for every Marine and thus doubly so for every leader. Unless you can confidently face your physical fitness test, you are not fit for active command." If there is a young boy out there wanting to be a Marine and I tell him "I am a United States Marine" well by golly I better look the part. I can pick a Marine or former Marine out of a crowd simply by the way he carries himself, and this goes for female Marines as well. My boys have followed my lead in their own way, one enjoys the sweat of a good weight room workout while another is a black belt in Tae Kwon Do and now pursuing additional martial arts disciplines.

The purity of the body is a central aspect of the triad and must be respected. This respect begins with treating our bodies as the proverbial temple with proper nourishment, rest and exercise. I am not advocating removing burgers and pizza from your diet, just remember, all things in moderation. Begin by setting the example, you might find yourselves pleased with the results. Age and gravity for those of us north of 50 takes its toll and is seemingly irreversible but this is not the case if we adhere to a simple workout and diet regimen. It's okay to have a cheat day or indulge in an ice cream sundae, just don't order the triple scoop with extra fudge and a cherry on top. Go easy with the soda, they have lots of sugar, and it doesn't help to order a triple cheeseburger, large fries and a diet soda. Really? Who are we kidding? Know yourself, know your strengths and know your weaknesses and work at your weakness until they equal your strengths; balance. If your son see's you sitting in front of the television with a king size bag of chips and an oil can of a soda, you are sending him a powerful message.

Spirit. I cannot overstate the importance of spiritual health or wellness, and this leg of the triad can be the most challenging for many yet, the most critical in times of great need or despair. We tend to defer spiritual health until faced with difficult times, and then we fervently re-engage with pleas for help. One definition of spiritual wellness is; "a personal matter involving values and beliefs that provide a purpose in our lives." We can include personal peace and harmony in this as well because when we are at peace with ourselves we are said to have spiritual health. Harmony is a deeper sensation of being at one with your surroundings or environment, being of harmonious purpose. This set of spiritual values that we develop helps to define us and give purpose to our lives. We may have a particular religion we participate in, or we may be agnostic but at the end of the day without a belief in a higher being or purpose we will wander aimlessly, missing out on the great beauty and harmony of spirituality. It is not the intent of this book to endorse a particular religion however, a bible based church is always a good source of spiritual direction. The old saying "There are no Atheists in a fox hole" holds true to my experiences and prayer can be a strengthening source of hope even in one's darkest hours.

While tending to my ailing mother during her battle with cancer, I had occasion to examine my spiritual strength very closely. To ask myself those very difficult questions of belief, an opportunity for deep introspection. Through prayer we learn about ourselves, through prayer we ask ourselves the difficult questions that we avoid in the consciousness of our everyday busy lives where we are more concerned with the material and the physical and not so much with the spiritual. My brothers and sisters joined in prayer at every opportunity, asking for her recovery, an expression of faith. I recall standing next to my Mom when she received the call from the Oncologist to inform us that based on the latest exam, she was cancer free. She wept out of joy, and although the cancer would return, she would live for another two years. Another two years which to her meant the world, another two years which to her was as if another lifetime. Two years later my Mother passed, I did not cry, and oddly enough I was not sad, I was thankful that her pain was gone, thankful that her struggle was over. I accentuate this event because in spiritual strength we find peace, in spiritual strength we find joy and in spiritual strength we find ourselves.

Taken collectively, we can see how powerful we can become when we ground ourselves in the foundation of this triad of strength. Mind, body and spirit must be proactively maintained just as an old classic car or it will begin to rust and fall into disrepair, destined for the scrap yard. I recall a moment of spiritual serendipity when I was in Saudi Arabia just before the attack into Kuwait during the opening hours of Desert Storm. The great battleships; USS Missouri and USS Wisconsin just finished sending 16 inch gun salvos at the enemy underneath B-52 bombers that were returning to base after conducting Arc Light like bombing raids and now artillery tubes were in battery and firing volley after volley at the enemy beyond the obstacle belts of minefields, burning trenches of oil and enemy tanks and artillery waiting for anyone who would somehow survive these obstacles. As the guns were firing, the sky was dark from the burning oil wells and the earth was rumbling from the great guns, I noticed a group of Marines gathered around a priest in white at the base of one of the guns, the padre was sprinkling holy water over their heads in baptism. Somehow the thunder of the guns was almost silent, my eyes were fixed on this display of peace and harmony in the midst of such extraordinary violence. This moment is seared into my mind and to me signified the importance of spiritual strength. These young Marines professed a strength of belief and trust in God that would bring them peace in the looming battle, serenity in the fires of war and the spiritual strength to persevere. Spiritual strength is surrendering what is beyond our control to the divine providence of the Almighty and to discover ourselves in the dichotomy of life's polarity, in other words, finding peace.

We know how to bolster the mind and body, there are tons of books on physical conditioning, diet and multitudes of fad workouts and diets intent on helping us to a healthier lifestyle for just a few bucks plus shipping and handling. But spiritual health is a much more personal journey. Don't get me wrong, there are plenty of books on spiritual wellness as well but I would wager that all things being equal; two opponents equally prepared physically and mentally, the one with strength of spirit will emerge victorious. Recall General Mattis' message to the 1st Marine Division "fight with a happy heart" this speaks directly to the strength of spirit the General was appealing to. To dig down for that intangible quality that somehow manages to overcome all odds and be the David that slew Goliath, the 1980 U.S. Olympic Hockey Team that slew the mighty hockey dynasty of the then Soviet Union. I could go on and on but you get the idea, spiritual strength trumps all.

My family all trains at a local martial arts school, Phoenix Martial Arts in Rockwall, Texas. We chose Phoenix largely in the same manner we chose our scout troop; we looked for a culture that represented strong family values, strong faith and a healthy lifestyle. The instructors, Masters Allen Smith and Gary Jones brought exactly that, and we have been training there for over seven years. The school logo is "God, Country, Family" and they provide a healthy environment we are proud to bring our boys into and proud to recommend to our friends and acquaintances. This environment makes it easy to address our mind, body and spiritual health needs in a proactive manner or what I referred to as "preventive maintenance." Find a place like this for you and your boy, it doesn't have to be martial arts, participate with him in something that gets you both out of the house, he'll likely show you up but the camaraderie you will share is priceless.

Now picture your son bringing all three strengths together, what a force to be reckoned with, what a pillar of strength. I have known many Marine leaders who live by this code, who lead by example, who live the life they expect their Marines to live because they know the value of this in combat – unstoppable. Fortunately for you, the Marines don't have a monopoly on mind – body – spirit, the power of the triad is yours for the taking, you need simply discipline yourself and your son to this lifestyle. Scouts place equal emphasis on this in the oath they take where they are called to be "physically strong, mentally awake and morally straight," and to "do my duty to God and my country." These words along with the twelve points of the Scout Law which include "A Scout is reverent," speak volumes of the emphasis we place on the development of mind, body and spirit as foundational traits of character and leadership development. Read, exercise and pray, pretty simple right? Yes, it is that simple, you need only allocate some time each day for a bit of each and it doesn't take much.

CHAPTER 17

ON HUMILITY

The bible has much to say about humility, in Matthew and Luke we find "whosoever shall exalt himself shall be abased; and he that humbleth himself shall be exalted." Many see humility as a sign of weakness while it is in fact quite the opposite. In a humble man we see strength and honor for the humble man does not seek recognition, nor fame, nor reward; the humble man simply does what is right, even when what is right may not be in his best interest. Humility is probably one of the most challenging traits to master and quite honestly, many of us will go to our grave confessing that we wish we could have been more humble in life. In humility we have to remind ourselves to be humble; when someone congratulates us on doing a good job, we respond with a humble "thank you, you are too kind," or "please, it was nothing." Being humble does not mean you cannot be bold in personal conduct or heroic in action rather, it simply means that you must not seek recognition, let it happen in due course… or not at all.

We often see interviews of sports figures after a big win, where the quarterback or the star player is brought before the podium to answer questions from reporters. Most of the time the star will speak in humble terms of himself and defer credit for the win to his teammates. Now, truth be told, most quarterbacks really believe they deserve all the accolades for a win, and none of the blame for a loss, but only the truly great one's really believe and understand in team sports, the collective team really is responsible for the win as well as the loss. I was once counselled that a good speech never uses the words "I" or "Me." If we have to point out how good we are, then perhaps we really aren't as good as we think.

We need look no further than pop culture where it seems to have become almost obligatory for famous music artists or actors to assume that their views on politics, world affairs and life in general hold more value and in effect, more meaning than the views and opinions of us mere mortals. The self-aggrandizement which seems commonplace at awards ceremonies void of any semblance of humility save for those few who choose not to participate. Ego is a powerful force and so, a very difficult force to control. Ego, together with greed are the prime ingredients for defeat.

My early childhood years were the era of professional football was really getting big. My personal favorite was Dallas Cowboys quarterback Roger Staubach. Roger was one of those rare breed of men that possessed extraordinary talent (Heisman Trophy winner) as well as academically gifted, (Naval Academy graduate) and if that's not enough he is also devoutly grounded in his faith. After graduating from the Naval Academy, he was drafted to play in the National Football League but unlike many star service academy grads who seek a waiver, he served his country in Vietnam. Any questions, refer to previous chapter on "Mind – Body – Spirit." I had the pleasure of meeting Mr. Staubach recently, one of the veteran's organizations I belong to; the Military Order of the World Wars was honoring him for his service to veterans. He personally funds an organization which helps place veterans in jobs.

Roger related a personal memory from his time in Vietnam. He said, "You know, I like you Marines, you guys are always out in the bush and always in the fight. I was just a logistician but I had a couple of Navy SEALs on my base in Vietnam and I would always see them all suited up for battle and go outside the wire, a few days later would come back all full of mud and grime. One day I went up to one of them and asked him;" "hey where did you guys go, and what did you do?" The SEAL looked me in the eye and he said, "Well Roger, I can't tell you where we went, but I can tell you we did a heck of a lot more than you." Roger, never one to talk about himself, chose to exalt the accolades of the Marines and SEALs in a self-deprecating way, humility at its best. He is one of the most humble men I have ever met and now in my eyes, even more of a leader.

Remind your boys that humility does not imply weakness, rather quite the opposite. Humility is a strength and should be practiced, and it should be practiced during the times and occasions least expected in today's self-gratification infused modern society. To practice bowing their heads in deference to their teammates, their friends and indeed to God. This healthy practice will not only serve to strengthen their character, it will also strengthen their reputation in the eyes of those that truly matter. Remind them to be gracious in accepting praise however, whenever possible, defer the praise to their teammates or subordinates. Not only is this the right way to conduct oneself, it will elevate his stature in the eyes of those that truly matter, those that look to him for leadership. Remember, humility truly is strength and should not be mistaken for weakness.

CHAPTER 18

ON FORGIVENESS

"To err is human; to forgive, divine." We've all heard this famous quote by English Poet, Alexander Pope from "*An Essay on Criticism*." His message is clear; that anyone can make a mistake, it is up to us to aspire to do as God does, show mercy and forgiveness. Isn't it so common that we hear of vendettas and feuds that last for years if not decades or centuries simply because we choose not to forgive. Perhaps we should consider the entry argument to forgiveness; "I'm sorry" if we assume that the person saying I'm sorry is sincere, then we should consider forgiveness. If on the other hand, the "I'm sorry" is not perceived as sincere then forgiveness should likewise be considered because to choose not to forgive harbors resentment, hate or anger. These sentiments and emotions bring negative energy and come to no productive end. Now there are many levels of offenses by which we must consider forgiveness, not the least of which are insults, rudeness or unwanted intrusions and span all the way up to physical attack or even death. At the end of the day, if we choose not to forgive, we will have burdened ourselves with resentment which only serves to eat away our sense of morality.

During my youth Scouting years my brother and I along with our Boy Scout Troop were on a Council wide campout in the hills just outside of Tucson. As is the case in campouts we had a nice fire built to gather around in the evening and tell stories, roast some hot dogs and just have a great time. My older brother Nick was sitting on a rock near the fire when a couple of

Scouts from another Troop came over asking if they could hang out with us. We happily invited them to join us around the fire. Now we were a small town troop and these other boys were from the inner city of Tucson but we were happy to enjoy their company. After a few minutes, the visiting boys left and we remained at our campfire to enjoy the evening. Suddenly we heard a loud "crack," we had no idea what the noise was but it sounded like maybe something in the fire had popped. Just seconds later my brother looked down at his arm and saw blood pouring down, whatever had popped had obviously struck my brother Nick in the arm. One of the older Scouts ran to get my Dad our Scoutmaster who was talking with other adult leaders while we bandaged up my brother's arm. Our Dad immediately showed up and packed up our troop and took us home. Before leaving, while putting out the campfire we found four more shell casings in the ashes.

When we arrived back home (about an hour drive) our Dad told our Mom "I have to take Nick to the hospital, he's been shot." Imagine our poor Mom's reaction! This was serious, it was a criminal offense and Nick had to give a statement to the local police officer. Understand the gravity of the incident; my brother or any one of us sitting around that fire could easily have been killed because of a careless prank. The next day Dad and Nick went back to the campsite to speak with our scout executive who informed them that the offending boy's scoutmaster wanted to kick them out of their troop. Dad asked Nick what he thought we should do. My brother's response was "If anyone needed scouting, it was them."

This example borders on the most extreme case of loss of life and although the example is absolutely pertinent to the topic of forgiveness, I hope you or your boys are not confronted with such a scenario. We can and must find forgiveness in all our hearts; we can learn to empathize with each other and understand what is going on in the hearts and minds of those who may offend or harm us. Sometimes, we must look beyond the act and focus on the bigger message of forgiveness like my father and brother did. Forgiveness is a choice, a choice that can make us a better person. Should the other person choose not to reciprocate with like sentiment, this is beyond our control and your boy may be proud that he made the right choice.

CHAPTER 19

ON VISION

Vision is not something typically associated with a young boy none-theless, it is an important aspect of their development. Without vision, there is no goal, without a goal there can be no path, only meandering. We too often see young boys wandering through life without direction, without ambition and without a goal for lack of the ability to estab-lish a vision. In cases where they do have a vision, they must also associate a plan to achieve that vision or it is simply a picture in the mind's eye without meaning or attainability, in essence a dream. Don't fret, some boys may find their vision later than others while some may at an early age believe they know exactly what they want out of life and might even have a plan in place to get there. Of course we are reminded of the old adage, "Want to make God laugh? Tell Him you have a plan." This is pretty funny but also pessimistic because regardless of the outcome, the planning process is invaluable.

We can establish that vision is the natural or God given ability to see within your particular field of view. Whether you are a boy, an eagle, a salmon or perhaps a giraffe you are gifted with a certain capability to physically see and unless you are an owl or a tarsier who have the rare ability to see 360 degrees (largely due to the ability to swivel 180 degrees at the neck) you are primarily looking forward. Now much to my amazement I discovered that my Mom and my teachers actually did not have eyes in the back of their heads. God, in His infinite wisdom decided it was more important to regard what is in front of us than what is behind us. In this same manner we should approach personal vision. Not so much the physical optical vision we use while driving or walking through the woods rather the vision we employ when assessing life's goals and aspirations. If the Almighty had intended for us to lament our past and brood over our failures in abject depression He would have given us those fabled eyes on the back of our heads (like my Mom and teachers). The past is for learning, nothing more. Until the time machine is invented, we can do nothing to change what has already happened and as difficult as it may be, we must maintain a forward focus to enable our power of mental vision.

We must also be able to relate and translate our vision to others. Consider the architect who is missing his drawings and must explain to his builder the type of project he must complete. If he cannot adequately communicate his vision then the builder will have no idea what he is expected to build. When you can communicate vision, you can allow others to participate in and possibly support your vision and goals.

During the summer of 2002 I was reassigned from the Marine Artillery Detachment at Ft. Sill, Oklahoma to the 1st Marine Division at Camp Pendleton, California. Understanding the timeframe, this was mere months after the terrorist attack of 9/11/2001. My assignment was to be the Targeting Information Officer for the 1st Marine Division. I would belong to the Fires Cell of the 11th Marine Regiment for accountability purposes however, my mission would be to plan targets for the division's operations. In November of 2002 after months of planning for what would be Operation Iraqi Freedom, the invasion of Iraq, I would deploy to Kuwait as part of the Division Forward Planning Cell. We had planned for months at Camp Pendleton, long days and some late nights going over intelligence reports and assessments, enemy orders of battle, terrain studies, establishing enemy most likely courses of action and most dangerous courses of action. My job, to assess enemy capabilities and develop targets by priority for engagement. Every unit in the division was going through the same planning process, it was at times mind numbing and repetitious. Our plan would change slightly and we would develop and wargame courses of action that we would possibly take. Using all this data and planning factors, we had to envision as best as possible what the enemy would do. The vision would then be transcribed into words and map products, even terrain models using tons of sand and Lego blocks to represent a visual display of what we saw in our mind's eye, (Valenti, 2014) . Planning, planning and more planning.

By the time H-Hour (the day to attack) arrived, we were set to execute the plan when a late night order from higher headquarters directed us to initiate the attack a good 12 hours sooner than planned. When you have 22,000 Marines and Sailors all synchronized to a certain plan and timing, changing this order at midnight is not typically considered a good thing. In spite of the late night, last minute change of plans, the division executed brilliantly and the battle would weigh heavily in our favor. My point; the plan may be thrown out the window at the last minute because things change, but the planning process is invaluable. This planning only takes place because someone had a vision. In our case, General Mattis conveyed his vision so clearly and so strongly that we all shared it as if we had a scope into his mind. The vision is useless unless we implement a plan to achieve the vision and the plan takes mental rigor, too often we give up on our dreams because we simply are not willing to do the heavy lifting to achieve our vision.

There is a child out there today who has a vision, perhaps the next Steve Jobs or General (Now Secretary) Mattis, or maybe the next Thomas Edison who will have clarity of purpose and knows where his life will take him. Our world faces many challenges, probably the most daunting is the looming shortage of, or access to fresh water. At first glance we might assume we are in for a global crisis, and if you research the issue you will find that many experts predict that future conflicts will be over water rights. There are current hot spots in northern Africa and in Asia where nations are already at war over water. There are people working this problem now and some of the ingenious ideas they have come up with would astound you. Water purification systems that can source a whole village with potable water with minimal energy requirements and low maintenance. Will your boy be the one to solve the next generation's problems or challenges? Will he be the first man on Mars or some other planet?

Encourage vision, but also encourage and nurture the entrepreneurial spirit required to build a plan to realize that vision. Encourage reading and dreaming; the imagination is the plow field of ingenuity and invention. Many of the science fiction movies dreamt up in Hollywood have now become reality and they all began in the mind of a dreamer, a visionary but remember, a vision without a plan is merely a dream. Introduce your boy to STEM programs, Science, (Technology, Engineering and Mechanical) where they will learn the tools of technology and stir their innovative thought. Encourage reading just for the fun of it because reading stirs the mind and stimulates thought. Give them an old radio or television to tear apart, who knows they might just fix it or even turn it into something we never even considered like a Star Wars type hovercraft, "May the force be with you."

CHAPTER 20

ON LOYALTY

This particular quality is one which bears close examination due to its demand for reciprocity. Unlike the dog which shows almost blind loyalty, where the "Master" need show very little loyalty to get almost complete devotion in return from his furry, four legged, canine companion. I can leave the room for 10 minutes and when I return it's as if my dogs haven't seen me for years, tails wagging, or in my case having a Boxer and an English bulldog (named Mattis), entire hind quarters wagging. In reality, our pets require a show of loyalty in return for continued loyalty from them, they just require less than people do. People are much more demanding or needy and will not offer blind loyalty without a like show of dedication in return. Loyalty is and should be a two way street and can be exhibited between friends, amongst co-workers or most especially in a senior – subordinate relationship where it is much more important for the leader to show loyalty to their subordinates, in essence "earning" their loyalty. The importance of loyalty cannot be overstated however, even more importantly, it cannot be abused and it should never be taken for granted.

Blind loyalty is one of the easiest ways to get yourself in trouble with one exception; loyalty to God. We all owe due diligence in matters of trust and allegiance before rewarding someone or some cause our loyalty. We can use many words which mean or infer loyalty such as respect, allegiance, trust, obedience and surely many others, ultimately they all lead to a form of loyalty. I have taken three significantly important oaths of loyalty in my life; one to my God in my confirmation of faith, one to my country in my oath of enlistment in the armed forces and finally to my wife in an oath of loyalty in marriage. Throughout life we may proclaim loyalty to people or causes however, the loyalties we swear to should be taken seriously, and faithfully executed. The bible teaches us of the brittleness of loyalty in the account of Judas Iscariot who would deny Jesus in his time of need for 30 pieces of silver. We are taught the exact opposite in the biblical story of Paul's complete devotion to Jesus after leading a life persecuting Jews as a Jailer. Jesus would confront Paul on the road to Damascus and this would change Paul forever. Paul's loyalty would prove unwavering even through extreme persecution by the Jews and the Romans, he took his loyalty to his death at the hands of Nero.

As a leader of Marines I had to understand the importance and gravity of earning the loyalty and trust of my Marines. In the Marine Corps, the trait of loyalty is developed through training alongside your Marines, building trust in your decision making, your tactical skills, your leadership and your devotion to them. Often this devotion means taking harsh action or discipline when your men are out of line. Loyalty demonstrated in times of adversity will fast track the reciprocal act of loyalty from your subordinates, you take care of them, they take care of you type mentality. In combat we more closely associate the word "trust" with loyalty because you build a sense of trust in your subordinates based on your performance, if my Marines trust me, they are more likely to show loyalty to me and if I am a leader of any measure, I will reciprocate with loyalty to them. This aspect of loyalty becomes all the more important when faced with life or death situations and instant obedience to appropriate orders is critical to the accomplishment of the mission and the very survival of your unit. We should also understand that loyalty has its limits; abuse of loyalty by betraying your companion's trust should void the reciprocity clause of loyalty. In other words; if I show up late for a meeting because the boss is my pal and I know he won't chastise me, then I have violated the reciprocity clause of loyalty and should fully expect a reprimand from my boss. Reference the story of Marine Staff Sergeant Jimmie Howard for an example of rock solid "two way street" loyalty between him and his men.

Another powerful example of loyalty can be found in the accounting of Medal of Honor recipient and Navy Seal Mike Thornton's actions in earning this prestigious recognition. While on a covert mission along with his commander and good friend Tom Norris and two Vietnamese SEALs, Norris fell grievously wounded. Thornton was roughly 500 meters away and one of the Vietnamese SEALs told him Tom was dead. Unwilling to leave his commander behind, Mike raced back to get his friend because, simply put, he knew Tom would do the same for him. When Thornton arrived at the body, he saw his commander had taken a bullet through the head and he could even see his brains. This would have killed anyone but somehow Norris was still alive. Thornton who is a hulk of a man threw Norris over his shoulder and fought his way back out to the beach where he towed the severely wounded Norris and one of Vietnamese teammates who was also wounded through the surf and out to sea on a makeshift flotation device. While dragging them all into the water Thornton himself was shot through the calf. They were ultimately rescued by a U.S. Navy vessel and Thornton refused to leave the side of his commander until he was sure he was in capable hands. By the way, unbeknownst to either of these SEALs at the time, Norris had already been nominated for and later received the Medal of Honor for a previous mission where he rescued two downed pilots behind enemy lines where it actually took him four separate attempts to save the two Americans. This is loyalty at a level many of us will never experience.

Can you earn the loyalty of your friends? Do they deserve your loyalty? Will they abuse your loyalty? Will you abuse their loyalty? All valid and important questions when considering loyalty. There are few guarantees in loyalty but we can take stock in loyalty to God with certainty of reciprocity. You should approach important relationships such as marriage with staunch loyalty, and if that loyalty is not returned, it does not justify abandonment of your loyalty principles. You must maintain the moral high ground lest your building block pyramid of values come tumbling down one after the other.

Instill in your boys a sense of loyalty and more importantly, what the cost of loyalty is, the effort it demands, the frailty of its continuity and the strength of its bond. Discuss with them how loyalty comes into play with friends and how to determine if loyalty has been betrayed and how to deal with such betrayal. Remind them that although they will experience occasion where loyalty may be violated, this is no reason to abandon one's principals which surround their sense of loyalty. Loyalty gifted to another or received from another should be vetted for integrity to ensure the reason for loyalty is valid and honest. Teach them that loyalty can be dealt out to many however, care must be taken not to extend loyalty cart blanche because it comes with a heavy responsibility as well as expectations and when offered in large scale put a demand for time and energy few of us have. Loyalty to God, country and family should have priority while friends and organizations will become wedged in between as time permits. We don't typically think of loyalty in terms of time however, life will bear this out to be true.

CHAPTER 21

ON ADVERSITY

Ah, adversity, challenging, difficult, dangerous, all adjectives which lend to the building of character. Too often we look at challenges as a deterrent, as an obstacle which prevents us from accomplishing what we want or need. We see the challenge and instantly assume that our task will fail or that our goal is no longer achievable, but then we make an attempt, even if halfhearted, and we begin to see hope, perhaps there is a way. Recall the story of Marine Staff Sergeant Jimmy Howard who had every reason to give up, every reason to believe that his mission was no longer achievable, yet he persevered, he fought on, he encouraged his men and in the end, he won. It is through these difficult tasks that we find out what we are made of, we find our true character, the mettle we are made of. We need look no further than our World War II veterans, in particular the Marines who fought against heavy odds and a dug in and determined enemy on Tarawa. Japanese Admiral Keiji Shibasaki bragged that the U.S. couldn't take Tarawa with a million men in 100 years. The Marines took Tarawa in 76 hours at a cost of 1,000 killed in action and over 2,000 wounded. The Marines attacked with such tenacity and speed that all but 17 Japanese defenders of the approximately 4500 on island were killed or committed suicide. This challenge almost defies the word adversity as insufficient to describe what the Marines faced, and yet they not only persevered, they won in the biggest way imaginable.

One of my older Scouts recently approached me and was concerned he would not be able to accomplish all the requirements for Eagle Scout prior to his 18th birthday which is the cutoff for making Eagle Scout. Now this young man had been an absolute superstar in the Troop and had all the qualities of a leader and more importantly the character we expect in an Eagle Scout. His concern was that the service project alone would be too extensive to plan, get approval and execute in addition to finishing up his remaining merit badges. He had a credible point, there was a significant amount of work to be done and very little time to do it but for him not to wear the coveted Eagle badge was almost unthinkable. We sat down and talked and after some deliberation and hesitation decided if he didn't try, then there was simply no way possible he would make Eagle Scout. If he did try however, there was a chance he could make it, but only if he truly applied himself. This young man, raised by a single Mom by the way, walked away with a sense of dedication and plowed ahead full steam. He made time between school, work at a senior care home, and extracurricular activities to plan and execute his project. We held his Eagle Scout Board of Review just three days before his 18th birthday. Adversity present, and defeated.

During our summer of 2015 trek at Philmont Scout Ranch, our crew of seven Scouts were faced with a daunting hike on day three. It would be a completely uphill hike for about seven miles with full packs and full water supply because the summit we were headed for at 11,700 ft elevation had no water source. On top of this, as we set out on our trek, a torrential storm began with lightning and thunder like the skies would surely fall upon us. The boys didn't even hesitate, they set out on the trail, much of which required us to climb on all fours with rocks and dirt sliding from under us with each step. This was a significant challenge for 14-17 year old boys, and I might add, a significant challenge for three 50+ year old Dads who were bringing up the tail end of the column. We huffed and puffed and muscles strained and burned but we trudged on determined to make the summit, failure or giving up was not an option. Finally, we reached the summit just before nightfall and set up our bivouac site, the Scouts had grown that day, grown in confidence, grown in stamina and grown in character.

If we fail to challenge ourselves, we will find life very simple, and very boring. Lewis and Clark would never have made it across the continent to the Pacific Ocean without the steadfast character and grit required to brave the elements and overcome the odds stacked against them. The fortitude of our founding fathers ensured the opportunities we all now enjoy as citizens of the greatest country on earth, had they succumbed to the overwhelming force and military might of the British Empire, we would all be eating crumpets and sipping tea (at a sizeable tax). Your boys have more grit than you may think they have, challenge them to put down the video game controller and to excel beyond their comfort zone, to seek out challenges and opportunities to test their mettle and you will surely be surprised.

The mere act of attempting something challenging is in and of itself a win because they have stepped out of their comfort zone. If we allow our boys to take the path of least resistance, or if we clear the path of any obstacles for them in the name of safety or because we feel that this is our role as a parent, then we have failed them. When the protective umbrella of Mom and Dad is pulled away, they will find themselves wholly unprepared for life's tough situations and at best, destined to a life of safe and uneventful boredom and at worst, a life of failure for lack of character. The next time you are tempted to intervene on behalf of your boy, resist the urge and instead watch or step away and allow him to pursue his mission. If nothing else, offer encouragement and let him try, let him fall and by all means let him fail because as mentioned in our chapter on failure, there is tremendous value in failing.

CHAPTER 22

ON CHOICES

D o I say "Yes," do I say "No," do I go up, do I go down? Our lives are a series of choices, most of them fairly trivial, but it only takes one wrong choice to send your life into a dismal spiral into the dark abyss. Only a slight exaggeration however, an important point of discussion. Now more than ever, our boys are faced with decisions with significant repercussions, this age of connectedness, of instant messaging and opportunity seemingly at our fingertips. In the old days we could draft a letter, read it, re-read it and re-draft it until we were satisfied that we had adequately communicated our message. Then we would put it in an envelope, walk it out to the mailbox (assuming we had a stamp) and wait for the mail carrier to come later that day or perhaps the next day. In all this time we had the opportunity to reconsider whether sending that message was the right thing to do. Today, our boys tap out a message on their phone and hit "Send" almost as fast as they finish hitting the last letter key. Having lived in the technology era for some years now, we are all familiar with that sickening feeling when we hit send on an important message, perhaps second guessing ourselves, maybe remembering we didn't check our spelling and grammar, or worse yet, that we should not have sent that message at all. As we say in the artillery world, "That round done left the tube," in other words, you can't get it back and what's worse is these electronic messages are digitally archived forever. So yes, choices today carry significantly more implications than in our day and it is absolutely critical that we teach our boys critical thinking skills in their decision making cycle.

While growing up I was faced with many temptations, and many of these temptations were in the way of drugs and alcohol. In my small town we didn't have much beyond your common marijuana or beer to choose from (at least as far as I knew), but have no doubt, the temptation was there. Because of my upbringing I had no problem saying no to drugs and my one time experiment with beer did not go so well. These choices would pave the way for me to be granted high level security clearances throughout my career and open doors that could otherwise have been closed such as guarding our embassies abroad. Today we see where teens are "sexting," wasn't even a word when we were growing up, experimenting with drugs that weren't even heard of in our day and now we even see the legalization of marijuana in some states. A simple picture on a mobile phone can go viral in seconds, a video on YouTube can make someone famous overnight, or conversely make someone infamous overnight. It all comes down to ethical decision making, our ability to make difficult choices, choices which challenge our level of understanding or comprehension. It is in these gray areas that our boys will be challenged and in these gray areas which require the most attention and character development because at the end of the day, it will be strength of character that enables our boys to make the right and often difficult choices.

There was an Air Force Colonel by the name of John Boyd who used his experience as a fighter pilot to come up with the OODA-loop concept. Perhaps concept isn't the right word but what he came up with was an astute observation of the human decision making process. First we "Observe," we take in what we can see, hear, feel or smell and this is the entry argument. Next we "Orient," we orient ourselves to what our senses have told us, the orientation introduces us to the decision making portal, our reasoning skills begin to energize. Next comes the "Decide," segment where our cognizant skills and knowledge come into play, the decision is based off our input from our senses, our orientation and finally our reasoning which drives us to enter the final stage of "Act." Action brings the whole cycle full circle and the minute we act, we re-enter the OODA-loop based on new entry data from our senses. I tell my Scouts and my sons that this OODA-loop is constant and repetitive even though we scarcely realize it. When we get out of bed and head to the shower or the sink, we have utilized the OODA process, when we see a penny on the ground and decide to either pick it up or leave it be, we have applied the OODA process. This process of making choices is learned and because it is learned, it can be improved upon.

In combat we apply the OODA-loop however, our intent is to get inside the enemy's OODA-loop, to out fight him, to out act him and most importantly to out think him. The greatest war time General of our day, General James Mattis was known by Marines as "Chaos" this was his radio call sign. Now many people would have you believe his nickname is "Mad Dog" but that title was bestowed upon him by the media. In combat and to the Marines that served under his leadership, the General was known as "Chaos." This call sign has significance because General Mattis' way of war was to get inside the enemy's OODA-loop, get inside their heads and sow chaos within their ranks, to use speed in action, deception and ingenuity to outpace and out think the enemy. This is the mark of a superior warrior, superior thinker and superior foe. The enemy will always find themselves trying to catch up, always reacting rather than acting because Mattis was one step ahead of them, he was in their OODA-loop, he owned their OODA-Loop. He made choices that he knew would supplant and undermine the enemy's plans. So you see, choices can have little to no consequence or they can be as significant as deciding the fate of nations. This topic bears more study.

Choice should not be confused with chance, for the two may at times be intertwined we should remember that chance is in the hands of someone else where choice remains solely with us. Chance may at times benefit our choices however, if we rely on chance we are no more apt to succeed than to predict the outcome of a roll of dice, the odds are against us. When our founding fathers opted to declare independence, they made a very calculated choice based on a myriad of facts and assumptions, much of which would imply just the opposite decision. Nevertheless, they chose to declare independence with the clear outcome of war with what was at the time, the mightiest military on the planet. The colonies did not have a standing army nor a naval fleet rather, we had what amounted to a ragtag group of armed militia newly christened as the continental army. What followed of course was the incredible defeat of King George's army and the establishment of the United States of America. In this case, passion, faith and frustration helped fuel a decision which most in retrospect may not have made but thanks to the bravery of a handful of patriots their choice was epically successful.

The choice of a single person can have profound consequences and we must assume that our young boys will at several times in their life be faced with the need to make difficult choices. Practice allowing your son to make his own choices, when he asks "What should I do?" turn it around and ask him "What do you think you should do?" Go over the facts, assumptions and potential consequences of his pending choice and then allow him to make his choice. If you, by virtue of life experience know his choice will end in failure, (but no significant harm) then allow him to go forth with his choice. He will be all the wiser for it, and you will have done him a great service in developing his critical thinking skills. The main objective here is to educate your son on how to make smart and ethical choices.

CHAPTER 23

ON ENERGY

T his is another one of my favorite topics because just the word itself gives power, hope, enthusiasm and many other good things we hope for in life. No, I am not talking about the energy that powers our refrigerator or our vehicles, not the energy that is nuclear, thermal, mechanical or chemical, but in a sense you'll see that the energy I refer to is even more powerful. Have you ever been at a party or in a meeting and when a certain individual walks in the room you can almost feel the energy level rise. This is that guy or that gal that somehow exudes that invisible energy that brings everyone to a higher level, to achieve beyond their perceived capabilities, to want to try harder, or just makes everyone in the room happier. This is the energy I am referring to and this is the energy we want to develop in our boys. Conversely, there are also those who bring bad energy, they drain everyone in the room, they make you feel like you need to take a nap. Have no doubt there are also those who bring an absolute bad and negative energy, these are those nefarious types who have high potential energy but it is all focused on bed intentions, and these types will try and drag you along with them.

When we think of energy, we should also consider its potential or what is referred to as potential energy. Imagine drawing back on an archers bow, when you have drawn it back to the arrow point, you have achieved its full potential energy. To draw it back any further would either snap the bow, or the arrow would fall from its arrow rest completely eliminating the usefulness of the energy. How do we know what the potential energy of our boys is?

How do we know how much potential energy they have stored up within them? More importantly, how do we nurture it, develop it and condition our boys to achieve it? Truthfully, we may not know exactly how much energy our boys have because they will likely not achieve potential energy during their childhood and this a good thing. What we can do is mentor them in the difference between good energy and bad energy and how they can draw from their internal source of energy for their life's goals.

As the 1st Marine Division crossed the line of departure in the attack into Iraq in 2003 our intent was to generate what we call "operational tempo" the result of speed and combat power. The 1st Marine Division known as "Blue Diamond" for its organizational insignia earned in World War II, a blue diamond with the numeral "1" centered and the stars of the southern cross inserted around the "1" and the name "Guadalcanal" inscribed inside the numeral "1" was over 20,000 Marines strong, with over 8,000 vehicles (tanks, armored personnel carriers, amphibious tractors, trucks, etc.) organized into three regimental combat teams. Our mission, to attack in force, defeat any opposition and destroy the 51st Mechanized Brigade of the Iraqi Republican Guard and additional brigades of the Iraqi 3rd Corps. This battle would be the longest land attack in the history of the United States Marine Corps and failure was simply not an option. In order to succeed, we had to generate an extraordinary amount of combat power and speed in maneuver which when combined equates to operational tempo. Now you can imagine that it would take some incredible coordination and organization to synchronize the actions of over 20,000 Marines and if any portion of our division was out of sync, it would have severe impact on the combat power and operational tempo of the attack; it would in effect substantially reduce the "energy" of the division.

As history bears out, the 1st Marine Division was successful in generating sufficient energy to defeat all enemies in our zone to include the 51st Mechanized Division, several Republican Guard outfits and culminated (so we thought) with the seizure of the Iraqi capital city of Baghdad. Imagine the amount of energy which had to transfer from a state of intense violence, to a state of relative calm when we reached Baghdad, all this happened through organization, synchronization and rock solid leadership. This leadership had to harness this energy, nurture this energy, and at the exact right moment unleash this energy much like a dragster taking off at the start line and then control it throughout the operation, violent and aggressive at first to send a powerful message to the enemy, then pull the reins when necessary to conserve energy for the next big fight, constantly monitoring the speed and power to ensure the operational tempo is synchronized with higher headquarters and adjacent units much like a maestro creates harmony in his orchestra.

In his Commander's Intent, General Mattis stated he wanted in part, "speed coupled with harmony of information flow, rapidity in decision making, response to changing conditions" and that "aggressive tempo and initiative are vital." All these aspects lend to the generation of energy of a military organization and at this point I should clarify the importance of harmony. Harmony in combat is the smooth and fluid flow of information and action synchronized with the speed of the force to create a steady and strong momentum, well informed decisions by commanders and subordinates alike and to create energy. His three paragraph commander's intent itself breathed energy and communicated a clear and powerful vision in the form of a word picture of what the General expected from the might and intellect of his division of Marines and served to allow his subordinate commanders to exercise initiative in the face of unforeseen situations and quite simply unleashes the natural aggressiveness of United States Marines. No enemy can stop this and we rolled all the way to Baghdad like a mighty wave.

No sooner had we begun to consolidate in Baghdad and taken stock of what we had accomplished than the order came down to stand up a task force to attack and seize Saddam Hussein's hometown of Tikrit. Once again, the generation of energy began all over again and Task Force Tripoli was organized and unleashed to attack in zone to seize Tikrit. General Mattis wanted to ensure speed and power so he assigned newly promoted Brigadier General John Kelly (now the White House Chief of Staff) to lead a task force comprised of three Light Armored Reconnaissance battalions and one artillery battalion named Task Force Tripoli after the historic attack led by Marine Lieutenant Presley O'Bannon from Alexandria, Egypt to capture the Tripolitan town of Derna, the first time the United States flag was raised in victory on foreign soil. This task organized unit would have close air support from the 3rd Marine Aircraft Wing and would swiftly and powerfully attack in zone to seize Saddam's home town within 48 hours. When you are able to generate immense energy, nothing can stand in your way, nothing can stop you and nothing or no one can defeat you. Imagine your boy harnessing such energy, it is entirely possible and achievable.

As with anything in life, there is a yin to the yang and we must be leery of the yin or dark energy and respectful of its polarizing pull. We can also look in our history books for examples of negative energy such as Adolf Hitler. Imagine the amount of energy it took for a former Corporal in the Austrian Army to rise to be the leader of the 3rd Reich! Beyond this, imagine the amount of energy it took to convince a nation that his way of leadership and his style of governance was in the best interest of the German people. So powerful was his energy that his actions started World War II and the deaths of millions of soldiers and innocent civilians, say nothing of the genocide and other atrocities. Hitler had reached his maximum potential energy yet he wanted more and he drew his proverbial bow back too far, he over extended the combat power of his army dissipating their operational tempo, essentially his arrow fell out of the arrow rest and his forces were defeated by the good intentioned and well-conditioned energy of the allied forces. We could compare the operational tempo of General Patton's 3rd Army to the operational tempo of Hitler's withering forces culminating at the Battle of the Bulge where Hitler sent over 250,000 German troops and hundreds of tanks in a last ditch effort to sway the momentum of the war in Europe. Patton's 3rd Army on the other hand achieved potential energy in punching through the German lines and relieving the 101st Airborne Division who were pinned down in the city of Bastogne.

We all know individuals who bring tremendous energy whenever they enter our midst, hopefully they are bringing good energy. These individuals tend to attract people, sometimes they attract both good and bad people however; bad energy will often reveal itself quickly and must be weeded out of the forum. The person with the good energy knows full well that the "hangers on" are drawing from his energy but that is intentional, he is using his energy to build relationships, to open doors, and likely to bring benefit not only for himself but for those he is endearing as well. Have you ever walked into a retail store and had a customer service representative approach you to see if they can help you? What kind of energy did this person bring and how did it affect your willingness to make a purchase? A good salesperson will bring strong energy and good product knowledge and likely make a sale while a mediocre salesperson will likely lack in energy and while their product knowledge may be on par with the high energy person, you are less likely to make a purchase. The high energy salesperson has their bow pulled back to full potential energy and they are ready to use it. This is the guy that sells you the new 3-in-one top of the line printer when all you came in for was an ink cartridge for your trusty old printer at home (I really like my new printer).

In the Fall of 2013 my son Gunner ran for Senior Patrol Leader of our scout troop. He maintained that he had plans and really knew what he wanted to do as leader. I watched as he campaigned and built his following up until the day of the election. It was a landslide, Gunner was elected as SPL and immediately set about instituting his agenda which was comprised primarily of building energy in the troop and making meetings and events fun. A stranger walking into one of Gunner's meetings would quickly be overwhelmed by the scouts running up front for recognition and returning to their seats amid a sea of high fives and cheers. The energy was palpable and to this day, many of the younger scouts, now older, fondly recall the days of Gunner's leadership.

Talk to your boys on a regular basis, learn about their strengths and weaknesses, what their dreams are and what their hopes are. Encourage them to pursue their goals with enthusiasm, encourage them to step outside their comfort zone from time to time if for nothing more than to get a sense of what they fear. Energy isn't always about having the "gift of gab" a mute person can have just as much energy as anyone else, it emanates from how they carry themselves, how they project confidence, how they walk, the body language they project and the fire in their eyes. My youngest son brings a quiet energy, he is confident, strong and intelligent but he much like my sainted mother does not feel the need to talk unless he has something that needs to be heard. My second son on the other hand projects his energy verbally and is very outgoing. During the American Legion luncheon to introduce the year's Boys and Girls State delegates, my youngest son was introduced as one of the Boys State delegates. The Master of Ceremonies gave a brief cameo of each delegate as they were introduced. In his typical manner, Cannon was stoic but confident. After the luncheon, the Mayor who knows both my boys quite well came up to my wife and I and said; "you know if that was Gunner up there, he would have grabbed the microphone and given a 20 minute speech on how great this is." Two dynamically different boys, both with high potential energy, just different ways of bringing it.

Encourage your boys to walk with good posture, nothing says "low energy" more than a teenager who enters a room with his shoulders slumped over, his head down and his hands in his pockets. How we carry ourselves is the bow string drawn half way back. Encourage them to use their strengths as a source of energy. In combat we establish what our enemy's center of gravity (strength) is and what their critical vulnerability (weakness) is and then we pit our center of gravity against our enemy's critical vulnerability. In the same token, your quiet intelligent boy should nurture his strength of intelligence and know how to project it as energy. If he astounds a group with an intelligent factoid while slumped over staring at his shoe laces and hands in pockets his intelligence will be lost before he opens his month. If on the other hand he stands straight, speaks clearly and delivers his insight confidently, bow string pulled back to the arrow point, he is more likely to emanate the field of energy he truly possesses. Mentor your boys in posture, confidence, body language and energy but have some fun with it. It's not enough to tell them what to do, show them how to do it. As Admiral William McRaven offers in his recently released book "Make your Bed, Little Things that can Change your life …and Maybe the World" doing something as simple as making your bed can set the tone for a day of success, even and most especially in chaotic times.

One last tidbit on energy to reinforce the "show them." I go to a kick boxing class six days a week and three of these classes start at 5:00 AM. I consciously come up with anecdotes, funny stories (and I have a lot of those after 28 years in the Marine Corps) and sometimes I'll just make up a story loosely based on my life experiences. The minute I walk in the door, I put a smile on my face, announce my arrival in a different manner each day and in a loud and confident voice. I have just raised the energy level of everyone in that gym, and I haven't even begun to have fun! Most everyone will give me a grumpy 5:00 AM look, some will return my greeting with a sarcastic but good natured comment, others will just look up and smile, waiting for what comes next. I talk throughout the entire class, addressing the group as a whole, then directing comments to individuals (makes them feel special), even throwing jabs at folks while they are doing push-ups or flutter kicks. They'll feign annoyance and throw a jab back at me, ah they are now building their own energy, it may be drawn from mine but that is okay, actually that is great! Remember, energy is constant, it transfers from one state to another. Once it reaches its potential, it does not simply disappear, it must continue, perhaps in a different state but continue it must. Take my energy, I am glad to share and I have more, much more.

CHAPTER 24

ON EMPATHY

I teach my Scouts that empathy is an important leadership trait and that it should not be confused with sympathy, it actually goes significantly beyond sympathy. Empathy according to Merriam Webster is "the action of understanding, being aware of, being sensitive to and vicariously experiencing the feelings, thoughts and experience of another of either the past or present without having the feelings, thoughts, and experience fully communicated in an objectively explicit manner." Therefore we can say that empathy requires a mature approach analyzing and understanding human nature and emotion given their surrounding environment and collateral influences. It is a form of emotional intelligence which allows us to interpret another's state of mind and act according to this interpretation, hopefully toward good ends.

When one of my sons was 12 years old we received word about the passing of my good friend's father. At the time, my friend was deployed to a hostile country and we were in the midst of trying to establish contact with him to notify him of his father's passing. He was aware that his father would likely soon pass before he deployed so this would not come as a complete surprise however, these are situations which should be handled with great empathy. My wife and I had to leave the house for a bit when my friend placed a call to our house phone. My son answered and immediately said "I am so sorry about your Dad's passing." Now this was a very mature thing for my 12 year old son to say and he had no way of knowing that we had not as of yet informed my friend about his Dad. In this instance, my son had an emotional understanding of personal loss however, he had not as of yet developed the empathetic understanding, the maturity of emotional intelligence to more delicately deal with the situation. Fortunately my friend knew this and was not upset, he actually appreciated the innocence and purity of my son's concern, and it turned out to be a kind way of hearing very sad news. How would your son handle something like this? Never easy regardless of age or maturity.

Empathy is one of the most critical traits of a good leader. A good leader must be tuned into the state of mind of his team in order to best apply his skills in a manner and time which best supports accomplishing the mission. Leaders will have subordinates within their organization that will be experiencing a multitude of life issues, emotional highs and lows, traumatic situations and many times they will not communicate them to you. This is where empathy comes into play; the ability to sense objectively the emotional state of your people and more importantly; how best to address them. A great leader will create a climate conducive to open and frequent communication. General Mattis probably exemplified empathy on a grand scale more than anyone I have ever met. His approach to leadership and mission was to create a "fraternity of shared risk and common vision" where barriers traditionally associated with leader – subordinate relationships were torn down to encourage a climate of inclusiveness based on skill, knowledge, capability and initiative. I recall the General saying to his staff, "I don't care what rank you are or how long you've been in the Corps, what I care about is what you bring to the fight." In essence he touched the emotional state of every Marine in the division who now considered themselves a crucial cog in the gear house of our operation. This is empathy at the doctorate level.

Use every opportunity to impart some wisdom to your boys, whether it is a situation on a television show or a real life event, quiz them on how best to interpret each party's emotional state and how best to apply the actions of a good leader using empathy and emotional intelligence. Use real life situations that you surely have experienced as both good and bad examples of empathy. Your boy will appreciate your openness and this type of dialogue shows him that you see him maturing and are taking an active role in his development. Remember, empathy is not the same as sympathy and we should ensure our boys understand that it is not merely enjoining in our comrades misery rather, it is understanding their emotional state and quickly instituting an act (verbal or deed) which may either lead them to a state of peace or at the very least to an improved state. At the higher spectrum of empathy, they will be able to understand and then motivate others to accomplish what they personally do not believe they can.

CHAPTER 25

ON BOLDNESS

Boldness appears at the onset of any meeting or introduction and is typically depicted in the manner in which we carry ourselves. Body language is the first indicator of boldness or lack thereof. We can see by how a young man carries himself whether or not he exudes confidence which is an ingredient of boldness but not altogether the full measure of boldness. We are all too familiar with the slumped shoulders, drooping head and hands buried in pockets of many teens and while this in and of itself does not imply a lack of self-confidence it does on the other hand run counter to the visual representation of boldness. Where self-confidence speaks to a surety of purpose or in knowledge, boldness takes this a step further and brings confidence in the face of possible danger. Boldness is a close cousin to courage where the main difference is boldness is primarily referenced in a moral nature such as "the gentleman approached the President and boldly spoke his mind without regard to personal retribution."

"Be bold, be brief and be gone." These words were "boldly" emblazoned at the entrance to the battalion command post at one of my Marine units. The implication, if you come into the Battalion Commander's headquarters, you should come in with purpose, with resolve and state your reason boldly, with brevity and not tarry about in idle conversation wasting people's time with issues on non-importance. Now there is always a few minutes to have some idle conversation but it should not consume the staff and distract them from the important duties they have. Von Clausewitz makes the comparison between courage and boldness in the following analysis; "where courage may be permanent or temporary, such as someone who is indifferent to danger which could be due to the individual's constitution, this can be considered a permanent state." In other words, this may indicate a sort of recklessness but it is a "dependable" state. The second form of courage involves boldness which is more of a temporary state based on such motives as "patriotism, ambition or enthusiasm." This temporary state of boldness is more situationally dependent and when combined with the first state of courage in an intellectual manner can be considered the highest state of courage. So you see, boldness as a character trait is of particular importance in a young man and should be nurtured and mentored along with courage.

Boldness, in the sense of a young boy must be bound by duty and a well understood sense of purpose, in other words, boldness unbound is dangerous and potentially harmful, so you can see where disciplined boldness can be an extraordinarily powerful force. Don't get me wrong, if I had to choose between raw boldness and timidity, I would choose boldness every time. Think back to the chapter "On Energy" if we can combine boldness with potential energy where boldness is disciplined and energy is loaded like the bow and arrow to its greatest potential, we can envision the capacity to accomplish most anything.

When North Korea attacked South Korea on June 25th 1950, President Truman needed an experienced commander capable of bold action to take charge of a fight that was rapidly being lost. General MacArthur came in quickly with a bold and risky strategy to land an amphibious force of Marines behind enemy lines at Inchon, cut off North Korean forces and their communications and supply lines. The enemy would not expect a landing at Inchon because of the danger involved in such a variation in low and high tides and even if such a landing was possible, the troops would have to scale high sea walls of large boulders and cliffs. The Marines would make this landing and the combined U.N. forces along with the newly arrived Marines would push the North Koreans back across the 38th Parallel in 15 days. MacArthur's boldness would pay off and would also cause the communist Chinese to enter the fight for fear of losing North Korea entirely. MacArthur's boldness would continue as he countered President Truman's peace proposal by taunting the Chinese and he even threatened to attack China. Now, I would be remiss if I did not also state that in no small measure, MacArthur's boldness ended up getting him fired by Truman, but had Truman chosen any other commander to assume command of the Korean conflict, South Korea would likely have fallen to the North. MacArthur rose to the heights and acclaim he did due in large part to his boldness in action, his disciplined and ordered approach to strategy and his ability to think big, never lose and never give up. Of note; Von Clausewitz opines that boldness when found in those of higher rank is all the more admirable because Generals out of the greater responsibility are bound more by intellect and temperament.

Encourage your boys to take the initiative not only in small things but in actions they believe to be insurmountable. This can begin with being bold in introducing themselves to adults, especially adults in positions of leadership. Shake hands firmly, look the person in the eye and say "Good morning Sir/Ma'am, my name is Johnny Jones, it is a pleasure to meet you." This is step one in boldness and will elicit immediate respect from the adult. Remember, boldness must be bound by intellect, by knowledge and by respect for the undertaking lest they abandon this and find themselves or worse yet, their subordinates in a dangerous situation. The boy that jumps off a moving train onto a slab of concrete may be bold but he is also reckless. The boy that jumps off a moving train and into a body of water or a pile of sand has bound his boldness with calculation. He may also injure himself however, he has calculated that the odds of success are far better than leaping off onto a slab of concrete. His subordinates are also much more likely to follow his lead.

CHAPTER 26

ON OPTIMISM

Ah, the glass is half full! Most teens don't have the problem of not being optimistic because they haven't yet been disciplined by life's realities. This is a good thing except when they place us parents in predicaments due to that innocent optimism such as "I'm gonna go to an Ivy League school," or "We want to do the 100 mile trek in 10 days." Everything and anything is possible to the typical teenage boy except when it comes to cleaning his room, taking out the trash, cutting the grass, cleaning the yard or washing Dad's truck. "How am I supposed to do that with everything else I have on my schedule?" So, yes, we need to address optimism.

When my middle son was 15 years old he went to Philmont Scout Ranch (two years before I went with my youngest) and the Scouts set about deciding which trek they would select. The boys had certain things they absolutely wanted to accomplish and certain portions of the ranch were much more conducive to getting these things done. For instance they wanted to summit Mt. Baldy, a 12,000 ft plus peak and this meant they would have to include the northern sector of the ranch in their selected trek. They wanted to have a day with the mules and this would prove more problematic than they anticipated. At Philmont each trek included a daily program which meant that the crew needed to rise early, prepare breakfast, pack their tents and provisions and set out to their next station which could be anywhere from 6 – 12 miles away. The program could be black powder rifle shooting, spar pole climbing, cave exploring, black smithing, rock climbing, rappelling and on and on for ten days straight. Keep in mind this was all at elevations of over 7,000 ft and often sustained elevations of 10,000 ft plus and almost always included uphill trails.

Well before departing for Philmont the boys held conditioning hikes (which in Texas would never come anywhere near 2,000 ft much less 12,000 ft.) Never fear, these boys had this in the bag. Well Philmont finally arrived and the boys began their trek full of energy and optimism. It didn't take long before they came face to face with Murphy's Law and how the littlest things can have a profound impact on even the best laid plans. When day 1 found them late for program, they had to conduct program the next morning which put them behind in hitting the trail that next day. Roll this forward and add in an average of 10 miles each day (if they didn't take a wrong turn) and you have a bit of chaos, but fun chaos nonetheless. This lesson came into play when my son and I helped plan our trek two years later, hence a tame 70 mile trek was selected and we truly enjoyed each day's program although we too had our moments with Mr. Murphy.

Nurture your boy's optimism, even if in your opinion they are too optimistic. Who are we to say that they cannot achieve their dreams? If your son lacks optimism, and there are those who do, help them build it through encouragement and confidence building activities because most boys who lack optimism also lack confidence. Dreaming is okay but remember, life's reality will discipline our dreams but that doesn't mean we should not dream big. Start by helping make their small dreams a reality, and educate them on how to achieve their big dreams through determination and persistence. Help them build a plan to get to that Ivy League school or to be a millionaire (then let me know how you did it). In doing this, keep in mind there is a fine line between helping and harming, allow them to stumble, fall and fail. Seriously, we all have the ability to dream big and we all have the ability to achieve those dreams, we simply find ourselves bogged down by the realities and priorities of life. Our boys can begin young, before too much of life gets in the way, help them to do this by clearing some of the thorn bushes from the path. We had a nightly ritual during our Scout campouts. Each evening before taps we would circle up and have each Scout give his Roses, Buds and Thorns or what went great that day (roses), what he felt he could improve upon or could have gone better (buds), and what was really just horrible (thorns), in his opinion. No one gets to refute or interrupt each boy as this is his stage and his book to read. Remember, every thorn can give way to a bud and every bud can become the rose, we just have to nurture it.

CHAPTER 27

ON LEADERSHIP

This book's culminating chapter on leadership brings all previous chapters together because if we think about our personal role models we can probably assess them to possess most all of these previous traits. Not every boy will grow into a leader but every boy will have the opportunity to lead. Some boys are born with some natural ability to lead but to be a truly good or even great leader, it takes study, practice and wisdom. By now you have no doubt my example of pinnacle leadership comes from General Mattis however, I had many great leaders who demonstrated the various levels and styles of leadership throughout my childhood and adult years. Who are your leaders? Who has been instrumental in molding and mentoring you as a leader or perhaps simply as a good person? Are you a leader? What kind of leader are you or have you been?

We should not confuse the difference between a leader and a manager; a manager manages processes while a leader manages people. Neither are easy however, to be a great leader requires emotional intelligence, the ability to interpret people, to understand the intangibles which must be addressed in order to motivate them to success. How do you motivate someone to do something he/she would otherwise prefer not to do? Can you keep a group of people focused on a task or mission while preserving their well-being and motivation? The ultimate test of leadership is in combat, hands down, because the burden of the leader is twofold, accomplishment of the assigned mission and the welfare (lives) of his men. A good leader will find a way to account for both. General Mattis used command and feedback as his approach to command; for a leader who blindly forges forward thinking his plan is infallible will soon wander off a cliff or into an ambush, or worse yet, may glance back to find that no one is following him. A leader must elicit the feedback of his subordinates and intellectually engage them to produce a better plan. At the end of the discussion, the decision ultimately falls on the leader (lonely at the top).

By its very definition leaders must be out front, contrary to what may be seen in many of today's so called leaders, one cannot lead from behind regardless of the rationale applied. During Operation Iraqi Freedom, General Mattis would depart the division command post each morning for the front lines because this is where he was able to observe the greatest point of friction and thus make the decisions expected of a commanding general in combat. In business and politics we can make the same correlation. The Chief Executive Officer or President of a company can no more lead from the confines of his office than a commander can lead from the security of his headquarters. Some of the greatest leaders in industry such as Jack Welch CEO of General Electric famously said, "Before you are a leader, success is all about growing yourself. When you become a leader, success is all about growing others." You can scarcely grow your subordinates from your executive leather chair. As Jack Welch states, a leader must grow himself first and this requires training, application, observation and more training.

These traits we have examined in this book by no means a comprehensive analysis however, provides you with the analysis and ideas to begin your training and application. You as the mentor can facilitate by providing your son with the opportunities to take part in organizations that provide your son with the opportunity to apply their new found skills as well as observe others, ideally their peers, also applying their leadership skills. During this process your son will notice traits or methods of leadership which he does not feel apply to his personal approach to leadership or his personality and this is absolutely okay. He will develop his own style of leadership and part of this is knowing what style or approach he does not like. This is the growth of the leader and it takes commitment, it takes courage and it takes purity of purpose. Remember, the greatest leader in history, Jesus Christ demonstrated servant leadership with one of his final self-determined acts in washing the feet of his apostles. We can all take a lesson from this regardless of our faith.

In my years of experience mentoring Boy Scouts I have come across a few young boys who truly had that natural leadership ability, they were a cut above and all the other boys fell in line behind them. Rarely was their leadership matured sufficiently to christen them pinnacle leaders however, they provided a good base from which to mold them further. Some were strong in knowledge, others brought great enthusiasm, while some had the ability to influence others (not always in a good way). So, the entry argument is to assess your boy's strengths and use his strength to bolster his weaknesses. For example, one of my Senior Patrol Leaders (SPL) had extraordinarily strong empathy and was great with the younger boys however, he was weaker in his ability to be forceful which sometimes creates a challenge with his peers. In such a case, we went to work on his command presence, his ability to project his voice, how he carried himself and how he should address the troop in an authoritative manner.

One of my favorites was my first SPL who was only 13 years old, was smaller in stature than his peers and did not possess a command voice however, he had the courage and confidence to enter the election for SPL. This alone spoke volumes of him and to my surprise (and even more surprised was his father who had no idea he intended to run), he won the election. We immediately went to work with structuring his meetings, discussing command presence, voice projection, and how to address an unruly group of 30 – 40 teenage boys. The length of time the SPL served was six months and somehow within these short six months the SPL had to establish himself as the leader, he had to organize and run weekly meetings, organize, plan and lead monthly events such as camping, backpacking, rock climbing, rappelling, rifle shooting etc. He had to resolve conflicts, address minor disciplinary issues and most of all, he had to keep the boys focused, productive and motivated.

At the beginning of the six months, his voice was somewhat low and had a bit of a quaver to it, his posture was what you would expect of a 13 year old boy and he surely doubted the wisdom in his decision to run for SPL. By the end of the six months, my young SPL was without a doubt in charge of his troop and when he stood in front of the troop during meetings, campouts or events, he had everyone's attention and he knew it. How did this happen? Through structured and consistent training, after action reviews of his weekly meetings and mentoring him along the way. My SPL would take every opportunity to attend local leadership seminars as well as BSA hosted leadership training. This same young man recently pinned on the coveted rank of Eagle Scout and the dynamic change and growth on display was absolutely amazing.

It is not my intent to endorse any particular youth program as every young boy should pursue a path which brings them joy and fulfillment. What you may surmise is my absolute endorsement of the opportunities Scouting can provide a young boy, the environment and culture is conducive to learning, failing and growing while having loads of fun. There are several other programs such as Civil Air Patrol, Sea Scouts, and of course the many clubs and athletic programs which provide our boys with opportunities to build character and leadership. Without these organizations we would find that our boys have missed out on key enablers to coaxing out some of the character traits we have discussed in this work. These organizations are staffed by volunteers, volunteers who like myself, have seen the wonder of a boy's eyes lighting up when they achieve, when they excel, when they are recognized and when they grow.

I have offered some ideas and recommendations on where you can send your boys for mentoring however, keep in mind that the primary responsibility falls on our shoulders as fathers, and in many cases as single mothers. In addition, there are organizations which invest an extraordinary amount their time, resources and capital into mentoring our youth. Our most precious commodity is time and as such we must be selective in how we invest our time. I have found that for my time, the greatest return on investment have been the American Legion who sponsor Boys State and Girls State as well as other youth focused events such as our local Post which conducts semi-annual Youth leadership Symposiums. All this at no cost to the individual or family. The Military Order of the World Wars which sponsors annual Youth Leadership Conferences for teens and recognize Boy Scout and Girl Scout pinnacle achievements; Eagle Scout and Gold Award respectively.

Consider if you are eligible, joining or at least supporting these organizations and if you are able to find an organization which contributes to the training of our youth then I highly recommend you carve out some time to join in and lend a helping hand, believe me, they will welcome the help. If you are unable, no harm, no foul, but don't let this prevent you from getting your boy out to experience what they have to offer.

One final story. Just this past weekend I was participating in a Youth Leadership Symposium sponsored by our Local American Legion, Terry Fisher Post 117 here in Rockwall, TX where we utilized John C. Maxwell's book; "5 Levels of Leadership" as a way to structure our training for the teens. Each one of the Instructors (all combat veterans who have transitioned to executive leadership in the commercial world) was assigned a particular level from 1 through 5 and tasked with a 30 minute session with a group of 6-8 teens. As each group would complete one level they would transition to the next level and a new instructor. Level 1 according to Maxwell is "Position" leadership or being the leader by virtue of one's position such as Squad Leader; you have to do what I say because I am in charge type leader. Level 2 is "Permission" where the leader learns the more challenging task of earning the right to lead. Level 3 is "Production" where the leader must motivate his team into being productive. Level 4 is "Developing" where the leader, now mature, must go to work in mentoring and preparing select subordinates to become the new leader/s. Finally Level 5 is "Pinnacle" where we find those rare and gifted leaders of industry, military and government who are seemingly the wizards of leadership. Well, we were about finished with our symposium so I walked over to watch the last group attend their Level 2 session (unfortunately due to time constraints we were not able to have each group attend each level in order) when the instructor asked if anyone had any observations or comments. One sharp young man raised his hand and stated matter of factly; "Yes, I can now say without a doubt that my parents are truly Level 1 Leaders."

EPILOGUE

Almost 40 young boys ranging between the ages of 11 – 17 gather round the cooking area, the cooks are almost finished preparing the meal and all await anxiously to partake. This was one of our bi-annual family campouts, a chance for families to come out and see what the troop was all about. One of the adults hollers "senior scouts first in line followed by junior scouts then adults!" The newly elected Senior Patrol Leader steps up and corrects the order, "Guests first, followed by junior scouts, then senior scouts followed by adult leaders, the Scoutmaster and I will eat last." Many adult family members had never participated in a camping event with their boys so they had not had opportunity to see the development of leadership in their boys. One parent approached me and noted, "This is amazing, I had no idea our boys had matured so much." Stick around I said, it only gets better.

After chow, the Senior Patrol Leader gathered his Patrol Leaders and staff and delegated tasks to be accomplished before the campfire that evening and then before lights out. There were dishes to be washed, camp cleanup, firewood and fire safety equipment staged and a designated patrol to coordinate the evening festivities. This all happened without a word from the Scoutmaster and with only minor griping from the boys (after all they are boys). The next morning as the adult guests were staggering out of their tents, the boys under the leadership of their Senior Patrol Leader and Patrol Leaders were putting away the last remnants of gear in the troop trailer and preparing to conduct a police call. Needless to say, the parents were not only amazed, but a bit ashamed as well, their boys had turned the tables on them and wouldn't you know they sure let them know it.

I hope you have enjoyed reading this as much as I have enjoyed writing it. If you are already volunteering in a youth mentoring program or organization then I congratulate you, if not, I encourage you to get out and join/volunteer in an organization of your choosing, you will find it invigorating, uplifting and highly rewarding. These teens have a way of transferring their energy to you (and at my age I can use it) and they always find a way to put a smile on your face. Our future leaders are out there today and this great nation will continue to breed men of courage and character, who much like a plant, need to be tended to, watered with wisdom, pruned of bad habits and nourished with guidance that only you can provide. Your investment is not only in our boys but also an investment in the future of this great nation. Move out and draw fire!

BIBLIOGRAPHY

Integritas Retrieved from https://asu06.wordpress.com/2010/03/15/the-origin-of-the-latin-word-integritas/ Accessed 3/12/2017

Heinl, Robert D. Jr., Colonel. Handbook for Marine NCOs. Naval Institute Press Copyright 1979

Jimmie Howard Retrieved from http://www.homeofheroes.com/profiles/howard_jimmie.html Accessed 3/14/2017

Lynch, Joseph P. Retrieved from https://www.dropbox.com/sh/sv12r3tlhwwg79v/AABJgl-H_5F-rqRLewIHe-Sxia?dl=0 Accessed 5/14/2017

Franklin D Roosevelt's First Inaugural Address Retrieved from http://historymatters.gmu.edu/d/5057/ Accessed 3/17/2017

Gunnery Sergeant Charles Restifo Retrieved from http://www.historynet.com/persian-gulf-war-us-marines-minefield-assault.htm Accessed 3/18/2017

Kosednar, Jackie. Stop the Fear, How to Train the Brain out of Fear Based Thinking Retrieved from http://www.themindfulword.org/2013/fear-based-thinking/ accessed 3/20/2017

Grossman, Dave. On Killing: The Psychological Cost of Learning to Kill in War and Society. Little, Brown and Company, Copyright 1995, 1996

Jason Rother Incident. Retrieved from https://en.wikipedia.org/wiki/Jason_Rother_incident Accessed 3/22/2017

Thomas A. Edison Papers. Retrieved from http://edison.rutgers.edu/newsletter9.html accessed 3/24/2017

Patriotism. Retrieved from https://www.merriam-webster.com/dictionary/patriotism Accessed 3/26/2017

LtGen John Kelly's Speech. Retrieved from https://www.youtube.com/watch?v=dGcV-iLti9_0 Accessed 4/1/2017

List of Most Viewed YouTube Videos Retrieved from https://en.wikipedia.org/wiki/List_of_most_viewed_YouTube_videos Accessed 4/1/2017

Patrick Henry, Give Me Liberty or Give me Death. Retrieved from http://avalon.law.yale.edu/18th_century/patrick.asp Accessed 4/1/2017

Schake, Kori N., Mattis, James N. Warriors and Citizens. Hoover Institution Press, Copyright 2016

Citizenship. Retrieved from https://www.merriam-webster.com/dictionary/citizenship Accessed 4/1/2017

Citizenship Military Service. Retrieved from https://www.uscis.gov/military/citizenship-military-personnel-family-members/citizenship-military-members Accessed 4/3/2017 Accessed 4/2/2017

Rice, Condoleeza. Democracy, Stories from the Long Road to Freedom. Copyright 2017 by Condoleeza Rice

Junger, Sebastian. Tribe, On Homecoming and Belonging. Copyright 2016 by Sebastian Junger

Civics. Retrieved from https://www.merriam-webster.com/dictionary/civics Accessed 4/3/2017

Honor. Retrieved from https://www.biblegateway.com/passage/?search=Proverbs+16%3A18&version=KJV Accessed 4/5/2017

Moyers S. Capt. Shore II, The Battle for Khe Sanh, Historical Branch, G-3 Division, Headquarters U.S. Marine Corps, Washington DC. 9. Library of Congress Card No. 75-603604

Gladiator. Retrieved from https://www.youtube.com/watch?v=jEMPyjATNC0 Accessed 4/7/2017

Boy Scouts of America Mission Statement. Retrieved from http://www.scouting.org/scoutsource/Media/mission.aspx Accessed 4/10/2017

Wooden quote Retrieved from https://www.brainyquote.com/quotes/quotes/j/johnwooden106379.html Accessed 4/15/2017

Spiritual Wellness. Retrieved from https://wellness.ucr.edu/spiritual_wellness.html Accessed 4/17/2017

Humility. Retrieved from https://www.kingjamesbibleonline.org/Bible-Verses-About-Humility/ Accessed 4/18/2017

Honor Retrieved from http://artofmanliness.com/2008/09/14/the-bushido-code-the-eight-virtuesof-the-samurai/ Accessed 4/26/2017

Loyalty Dunbar number Retrieved from http://www.newyorker.com/science/maria-kon-nikova/social-media-affect-math-dunbar-number-friendships Accessed 4/28/2017

Tom Norris Retrieved from http://www.cmohs.org/recipient-detail/3374/norris-thomas-r.php Accessed 4/29/2017

Norris, Tom. Thornton, Mike. Couch, Dick. By Honor Bound. Two Navy Seals, The Medal of Honor, and a Story of Extraordinary Courage. St Martins Press, May 2016

Looming Water Crisis Global Researcher Feb 2008 Retrieved from. www.globalresearcher.com Accessed 5/1/2017

Adversity Battle of Tarawa Retrieved from. http://www.history.com/topics/world-war-ii/battle-of-tarawa Accessed 5/2/2017

Boyd's OODA loop, Richards, J. Addams & Partners, March 21, 2012

History in the Headlines. The Battle of the Bulge. Retrieved from http://www.history.com/news/8-things-you-may-not-know-about-the-battle-of-the-bulge Accessed 5/4/2017

McRaven, William H., Admiral. Make Your Bed. Copyright William H McRaven, 2017

Empathy Retrieved from https://www.merriam-webster.com/dictionary/empathy Accessed 5/5/2017

MacArthur Retrieved from http://www.crf-usa.org/bill-of-rights-in-action/bria-17-3-b-truman-macarthur-and-the-korean-war.html Accessed 5/10/2017

Maxwell, The 5 Levels of Leadership, Maxwell, 2011